GUIDE TO THE
Wines
OF THE
United States

Dominick Abel

CORNERSTONE LIBRARY
New York

Designed by Irving Perkins
Manufactured in the United States of America

Library of Congress Catalog
Card Number: 79-51951

ISBN 0-346-12427-1

FOR MY FATHER

Acknowledgments

I owe a debt of thanks to all those who, over the years, have shared information, experiences, and glasses or bottles of wine. Of particular assistance, in terms of this book, have been The Wine Institute, especially Brian St. Pierre, and Marjorie Lumm of the Monterey Winegrowers Council and Millie Howie of the Sonoma County Wine Growers Association. To these and all others I extend my thanks.

CONTENTS

1

WINE IN THE UNITED STATES
A Brief Account

The vines Leif Ericson encountered when he visited North America some one thousand years ago may not have been grapevines. But he was on the right track when he called the land he discovered "Vinland." As the land's earliest settlers soon recognized, the United States is a winegrower's paradise. The climate, not to mention the soil, in many parts of the country is ideal for grapegrowing; in some places—chief among them California—the climate for grapegrowing is unmatched anywhere in the world.

American settlers and farmers were quick to discover their good fortune. As early as the mid-sixteenth century—Leon D. Adams, the chief historian of the U.S. wine industry, has found—settlers were making wines from the native Scuppernong grape in Florida. Since that time, efforts to grow grapes of all kinds—especially the *Vitis vinifera* varieties that grow in and have made famous the wines of France, Germany, Italy, and other European nations—have been continuous.

At first, the only grape that grew and produced well was the Scuppernong. This grape, which belongs to the *Vitis rotundifolia* (muscadine) group of vines, grows predominantly in the Southeast, from Florida to Tennessee and from Virginia to Mississippi. It is a true native American grape, growing wild before being domesticated in the humid lowlands of the Southeastern states. It produces a pungent, aromatic, and very strongly flavored wine of no particular distinction but great weight.

In the early twentieth century a Scuppernong blend called Virginia Dare became the most popular wine in the country, and the wine's producer became a very wealthy man.

Virginia Dare's inventor and the man who named the wine, Paul Garrett was an avid promoter of wine use, even during Prohibition. He bestowed upon himself the title "captain," and no one begrudged him it. During that period he sold Vine-Glo, a wine juice concentrate used for home winemaking, Virginia Dare wine tonic, and other wine products, all the while crusading for the repeal of Prohibition and the promotion of American wines.

Captain Garrett was neither the first nor the last great character in the wine business—nor the only person to make a fortune—but in his enormous enthusiasm for wine he was typical of many who have worked to produce, promote, and sell wines in the United States.

THE DISCOVERY OF VITIS LABRUSCA

One of the more important early figures was a Revolutionary War winegrower, the gardener of John Penn, lieutenant governor of Pennsylvania. Although the name of John Alexander is to be found only in books on agriculture, his contribution to his country was significant, for he first discovered the *Vitis labrusca* grape, recognized it as a natural hybrid, and domesticated it. The merits of this new vine, the Alexander, were immediately apparent.

The Labruscas solved the major problems of those who were trying to grow European vines in the United States. These vines were found to be markedly resistant to vine disease and vermin as well as to the cold winters of the northern states—conditions that had jointly or singly, but always with speed, put an end to earlier efforts to introduce *Vitis vinifera* vines to the colonies.

The discovery and propagation of the Labruscas—Alexander, Concord, Isabella, Catawba, and their like—marks an important milestone in the development of the U.S. wine industry. The Scuppernong relishes a hot, damp climate; defying proper cultivation, it just grows. But the Labruscas are real vines. To the delight of many an American farmer, they can be propagated and grown scientifically and readily in a large variety of locations.

By the middle of the nineteenth century Labruscas were growing, and wine from them was being produced, in most middle Atlantic, midwestern, and southern states. The unique taste of Labrusca wines, which usually is described as "foxy," had become *the* taste of American wines, the standard against which other wines were judged.

As the cultivation of Labruscas spread, Ohio became the chief wine-producing state, with Cincinnati its capital. It was outside Cincinnati, on the banks of the Ohio, that Nicholas Longworth, another great character in the story of American wine as well as in the story of Ohio, planted his Bald Hill vineyard in 1823.

Longworth, a young easterner who had heeded the call to go west at an early and unpromising age—he had little to go west *with* and nothing to go west *to*—had through hard work and good fortune become immensely wealthy. Longworth's grapegrowing, at first the whim of a wealthy eccentric, soon became an obsession. Concentrating on the Catawba—developed in Georgetown in 1823, the year Longworth began his Bald Hill operation, and soon introduced to this property—Longworth produced a variety of wines, including a sparkling Catawba. The fame of his wine, the first U.S. sparkling wine spread to Europe, and Longworth's wines were shipped to practically every part of the United States. His Catawba even inspired Henry Wadsworth Longfellow to write his "Ode to Catawba Wine."

The first stanza of this poem, which can hardly be called a literary gem, reads:

> *Very good in its way*
> *Is the Verzenay*
> *Or the Sillery soft and creamy;*
> *But Catawba wine*
> *Has a taste more divine,*
> *More dulcet, delicious, and dreamy.*

The Cincinnati vineyards were eclipsed in the 1850s and fell into a state of total disrepair, from which only today are they recovering in a small way. One problem was disease, which struck savagely and without respite; the other was the growth of competing vineyards. One newly discovered section lay within Ohio itself: the south shore of Lake Erie and the coastal islands just offshore. This industry, which was centered on the little town of Sandusky, survives and flourishes today, despite competition and Prohibition.

The Sandusky-Lake Erie wine industry, significant though it was, never achieved the same dominance as Cincinnati. Leadership in the wine world was assumed instead by a state that, to us today, would seem a most unlikely candidate—Missouri. In Civil War times, the Missouri industry, under the leadership of George Hussmann, was the single most important producer of wines. But it remained supreme for only a short period. Blight and the growing influence of the drys, the benighted proponents of Prohibition, conspired to destroy the Missouri industry before it had a chance to develop staying power.

That staying power is necessary to survival is amply demonstrated by the story of winegrowing in New York. Today the leading nonwestern producer of wines in the country, New York has a history of winemaking littered with conflicts.

Wine and New York State have been associated for several hundreds of years. Vines grew in Manhattan in the days of Peter Stuyvesant, and an infant industry had established itself in the Hudson Valley before the middle of the nineteenth century. The oldest winery in the United States is in the Hudson Valley, the Brotherhood Winery, though it no longer grows its own grapes.

Hudson Valley winemaking was never a matter of great significance. The first breakthrough in New York occurred when winemaking was introduced to Chautauqua County in the far west of the state, on the shores of Lake Erie.

Ironically, Chautauqua County was also a stronghold of the drys. There, toward the end of the nineteenth century, led by Charles Welch, a local dentist and fanatic Prohibitionist, the drys mounted a struggle of hitherto unknown intensity. It was there, in 1873, that the Women's Christian Temperance Union was born; and there, too, that the Concord grape was introduced, not to serve as a new source of wine, but to supplant vines that could be used only to produce winegrapes. The Concord fed the infant but voracious grape jelly and juice industries spawned by the drys in direct competition with wine producers. In about 1860, commercial wine production in New York began in and around Chautauqua County. At roughly the same time, operations began in what became New York's premier wine-producing area, the Finger Lakes region, in west-central New York. In 1860, at Hammondsport, the Pleasant Valley Company opened its doors, producing wines under a label that still has an honorable name today: Great Western.

Over the course of the hundred years or so since the founding of Pleasant Valley—a progress interrupted only by the rude and very nearly disastrous shock of Prohibition—the New York wine industry has solidified its claim to be considered the premier producer of Labrusca wines in the nation. This is no mean peak to have scaled and remained atop, yet the New York industry is a midget compared to that of California, the development of which has followed a course very different from that of the wine industry of the East.

Today California produces about three-quarters of all wine drunk in the United States, and its share of domestic production is even higher. Some 80 percent of all wines produced in North America comes from California.

CALIFORNIA

The reason for California's predominance can be summed up in one word: climate. California offers the grapegrower opportunity presented nowhere else in the world, and it is to the West's climate that the unique story of West Coast wine is attributable. Because of the weather, the *Vitis vinifera* vines that doggedly refused to grow in the East and Midwest grew prolifically in the West.

The Spanish conquerors introduced the *Vitis vinifera* vines to the New World. As early as the seventeenth century, missionaries in what became known as New Mexico had established a not particularly noteworthy Vinifera, the Mission vine, to ensure a ready supply of wine for religious purposes. About a hundred years later, the Mission was brought to San Diego, California, for the same reason.

The practice of viniculture was introduced at each of the missions that the Franciscans of Mexico, led by the redoubtable Fr. Junípero Serra, established along the coast of California. The missions stretched between Sonoma, in the north, and San Diego, in the south. Thus, when the monasteries were secularized in the early nineteenth century, a viticultural tradition and, even more important, familiarity with basic vinicultural methods were already established.

Almost at once commercial wine production made an appearance, and its potential was quickly appreciated. By 1830 wine made from better-quality Vinifera vines, imported from Europe, was being made in quantity, and with style, in Los Angeles.

The California industry grew so fast that in a few years California wines were being shipped not just to New York and the East but also to Europe and as far as Russia. Only France resolutely set its face against California wine, a stance from which it has never relented.

In the midyears of the century, the jewel of California, the North Coast Counties, began serious production of wines. Popular credit for this is usually given to Agoston Haraszthy, to whom we will come shortly, but an even more important role was played by General Mariano Vallejo, the Mexican government's regional governor. In 1834, when the Sonoma Mission was abandoned, Vallejo bought the mission's vineyards, thereby ensuring that winemaking would continue in the area.

Others joined Vallejo—among them Jacob Gundlach, a German winemaker whose name has recently been revived as part of the title of Gundlach-Bundschu Winery. But Sonoma did not really blossom as a wine area until the arrival of Count Agoston Haraszthy, who first visited Sonoma in 1856.

Haraszthy, a Hungarian adventurer and founder of Sauk City in Wisconsin, was as much entitled to his title as Garrett was to his. Typically, he was a man of volcanic energy. Falling in love with Sonoma, he transplanted his vines from San Mateo, where he was having no success making wine, and established himself in style at a place he called Buena Vista. There he quickly became Sonoma's and California's champion and General Vallejo's chief (but friendly) rival.

In the latter category Haraszthy was less successful than in the former. His two sons married the general's two daughters, and Vallejo's wines were generally considered superior to Haraszthy's. In the former arena, though, he made a great contribution. After writing widely in praise of California grapes, he finagled a trip to Europe in 1861 as the personal representative of the state of California. When he returned, he brought with him over one hundred thousand vines, the proliferation of which led to the establishment—incorrect, as we have seen—of his reputation as the father of Vinifera winegrowing in California and to the substantial upgrading of California's vine stocks.

In the middle 1860s, Haraszthy, always an intemperate and impatient man of immense vision, fell foul of his bankers and his ambition. In a rage he departed California for Nicaragua. There he disappeared from view, having in all likelihood been eaten by an alligator.

Haraszthy was a comet, and if he is not the father of California viticulture, he was a supremely successful popularizer. His efforts helped stimulate the development of vinegrowing in the whole North Coast Counties region. In Haraszthy's time, for example, his European imported vines, for which he was never paid by the state, were scattered about California, and the attention he focused on the region helped bring Napa Valley, slightly to the east of Sonoma and destined to become the finest wine-producing region in the country, to the fore.

California vineyards—for that matter all U.S. vineyards—received a terrific boost in the last quarter of the nineteenth century as vineyard after vineyard in Europe was devastated by the *Phylloxera vastatrix*, a vine pest, which arrived with U.S. vines brought to Europe for experimental purposes. Had it not been discovered that the hardy midwestern vine root was immune to the ravages of this vine louse, the whole European industry would have been brought to its knees. As it was, European winemakers were faced with wholesale devastation and loss; and even though growers replanted as quickly as possible with midwestern vine roots—many supplied by George Husmann of Missouri—and then grafted their precious fine vines to this common stock, California was given an unexpected opportunity to show its paces. California's triumph would have been less Pyrrhic had growers not belatedly discovered that phylloxera, no respecter of national boundaries, was meanwhile also decimating the California vineyards. To this day, in Europe and the Western world almost all quality vines are grafted onto lowly but hardy midwestern roots as protection against phylloxera.

As Americans recovered from the phylloxera attack, the wine industry surged into its first heyday. California was coming into its own as the golden state of wine. Publisher George Hearst owned four hundred acres in Sonoma at his death in 1891. Robert Louis Stevenson called Napa wines in 1880 "bottled poetry." New York's Finger Lakes and other wine-producing areas were earning acclaim, especially for their sparkling wines. A measure of the level that U.S. wines had reached can be taken from the international wine competition held in conjunction with the 1900 Paris Exposition. More than two dozen California wineries, including such now-familiar names as Paul Masson, Italian Swiss Colony, and Beringer Brothers, won medals; even more significantly, perhaps, so did wines from Washington, D.C., Ohio, Virginia, North Carolina, Florida, New Jersey, and New York.

The future should have been rosy; the job of the winemakers seemed to be merely to improve and expand. But already there was visible, way above the horizon, a cloud far bigger than a man's hand: The specter of Prohibition loomed constantly larger and more overbearing.

PROHIBITION AND ITS AFTEREFFECTS

The Prohibition movement has a history almost as long as the wine industry in the United States. As early as 1816, one state, Indiana, had passed a law prohibiting the sale of alcoholic beverages on Sundays, the first statewide dry victory. As the century passed, the drys felt more and more strongly that they not only could win the battles but also would win the war. One by one communities voted themselves dry under pressure from crusaders. Whole states followed suit, with Kansas leading the way in 1880 behind the banner of Carry Nation. States that remained wet, such as New York, witnessed increasingly vehement struggles until the wets capitulated nationwide. Nineteen nineteen saw passage of the well-intended but highly injurious Eighteenth Amendment. Prohibition was the law.

Europeans looked on, amazed, at the madness of America, and European winemakers, though deprived of an important market, gloated as winery after winery shut its doors and uprooted its vines or struggled to stay alive as a supplier of sacramental wines or through some such scheme as Captain Garrett's Vine-Glo. The small loophole in the Prohibition law that allowed individuals to make up to two hundred gallons of wine for their own consumption did little more than keep a few wine-drinking traditions alive.

The 1933 repeal of Prohibition raised the curtain on an industry severely, if not mortally, wounded. Unfortunately, for winemakers and consumers alike, no one benefited from the industry's overall reaction to the return of sanity. Because decent wine was virtually unobtainable for the thirteen years closely following the war years, many Americans had come of age knowing nothing of wine's charms. During Prohibition, too, much fine wine acreage had been converted to cultivation of lesser varieties of grapes, and many wine experts had left the industry never to return. Growers were woefully unprepared for the repeal of Prohibition—a patchwork affair, since many communities and some states remained dry.

This combination of conditions resulted in most wineries' producing sweet, fortified wines with relatively high alcoholic content (20 percent) as a way of getting rid of their products and exploiting the market that existed. This wine tasted awful, but it was cheap to produce and could therefore be sold inexpensively. As "port" and under various brand names, this sweet wine slaked the thirst of innumerable inhabitants of the nation's skid rows and was sensibly reviled by most more fortunate Americans. Ironically, by doing its best to destroy the budding table wine industry in the United States, the drys had fostered alcoholism.

The way out of this slough was long and arduous; it required perseverance and not a little faith. Fortunately, winemaking always attracted persons of will and enthusiasm, and quality wine production did not die. In the 1930s the seeds of renewal were sown.

Among the most important developments during this period was the work of a Maryland journalist and amateur wine enthusiast, Philip Wagner, who developed for the American market the first French hybrid vines—crosses of Vinifera and Labrusca vines that produced hardy wines showing little or no trace of Labrusca foxiness. From the first vines Wagner grew have come many fine wines now known as Seyval Blanc, Chelois, Aurora, and Baco Noir, to name only a few.

As the hybrids spread over the East and Midwest, quality producers in the West discovered that a small market for their wines continued to exist. Wineries such as Beaulieu, for example, held by one family from its founding in 1900 until 1969, made commitments to quality to which they held unswervingly, and a small public responded.

THE PRESENT

The small public grew larger after World War II. The affluence of the postwar years, increasing European travel by Americans resulting in exposure to the pleasures of table wine, plus the developing sophistication of the U.S. consumer gradually convinced winemakers and the business world that the table wine market was real and growing.

In the mid-1960s, the table wine market surpassed the sweet wine market. At that point, producing wines for the "ordinary consumer" became more important than producing wine to be retailed as cheaply as possible. Table wine sales have continued to spiral. This statistic indicates that table wine consumption is growing steadily and that, therefore, there is little chance that the industry will return to the "bad old days."

One story, small but symptomatic, sums up most of the change. No one is prouder of his national wines than a Frenchman, often with good reason. A Frenchman's usual reaction to the notion that fine wine can be and is made in America is at best a condescending smile and at worst a blast of derision. Thus when a young wine store proprietor in Paris, Stephen Spurrier, decided, in May 1976, to hold a blind tasting of, on the one hand, six California Cabernet Sauvignons and six California Chardonnays and, on the other, four classified red wines from Bordeaux and four great white wines from Burgundy, there was little doubt how the judging would go, especially since the judges were expert *and* French.

In fact, the results were unprecedented, and very embarrassing to France. In the red wine category, American wines came in first (Stag's Leap Wine Cellars 1973), fifth, eighth, ninth, and tenth. In the white wine competition the Americans did even better, coming in first (Chateau Montelena 1973), third, fourth, sixth, ninth, and tenth.

In wine circles much too much has been made of the U.S. showing. The Spurrier tasting does not prove anything beyond the relative showing of certain French and U.S. wines. But by the same token, modesty and reason should not lead one to underestimate the strides that quality U.S. producers have made in very recent years. If the Spurrier tasting proved nothing else, it proved that U.S. wines have finally come of age.

A brief statistical survey of the size of the industry shows that this recognition is belated. In 1977, for the first time, the U.S. industry sold in excess of 330 million gallons of U.S.-produced wine, the market having grown at an annual rate of 19 percent since 1972. In 1978 the Bank of America forecast that consumption would rise at the rate of 6 percent per year—other estimates are higher—until the mid-1980s, having already risen from 1.52 gallons per adult capita in 1960 to 2.75 gallons in 1976. In 1978 there were about 350 wineries in California and more than 600 in the entire United States; new wineries were getting themselves bonded practically weekly; and the retail wine business was valued at three billion dollars. The statistics are endless. The point is easily made: the quantity of U.S. wine business is significant.

It is surprising, in view of the size of this behemoth, that it took something like the relatively insignificant Spurrier tasting to focus attention on the strides that have been made. What they were and what they mean—and what is lacking—are questions this book addresses.

2

VINES AND WINES

Although the U.S. wine industry began, to all intents and purposes, with the Labrusca grape and although these and their cousins, the French hybrids, still are cultivated in the East, Southeast, and Midwest, California produces the bulk of today's wine. Indeed, even non-California producers make use of substantial quantities of California wine in the making of many of their wines.

If many of the states are hospitable to the vine, none is so happily endowed as California. In particular, no other state can grow *Vitis vinifera* vines as California can, and it is the wines produced from Vinifera grapes that most of the world is talking about when it speaks of wine.

Given California's supremacy—and the fact that California wine types conform to the international norm—in any survey of the chief wines produced in the United States, one must start with its Vinifera wines. Many Vinifera vines are cultivated, but we need concern ourselves only with the major varieties. The term *varietal* is used to denominate a wine that is composed, in fact or for regulatory purposes, of wine made from one type of vine.

RED VINIFERA WINES

Cabernet Sauvignon

This is the name of the most famous red wine grape produced in California. Cabernet Sauvignon is the chief grape of Bordeaux, and California Cabernet Sauvignons are similar in style to the red wines of Bordeaux. Wines made from this grape have a distinctive perfume. They are very-dark-colored wines, and the best are either big, intense, tannic, and oaky or soft but firm, light-bodied, and elegant. The cheaper Cabernet Sauvignons are aged for two years in barrels, can be drunk immediately, but will improve for a year or two in the bottle. The more expensive ones have usually been aged longer and need another few years in the bottle before being drinkable.

"Bottle aging" allows wines to develop their velvet subtlety to the full. The tannin, detectable in good, young Cabernet Sauvignons, dissipates with age, allowing the wines to demonstrate their complex, superb flavors, which are often likened to eucalyptus or black currants.

Making a good Cabernet Sauvignon requires fine grapes, a high degree of skill, and refusal to compromise one's standards. For these reasons alone, Cabernet Sauvignons cost more than other California wines.

Pinot Noir

Pinot Noir is the second great red wine grape of France, where it is the sole component of the red wines of Burgundy. Its history in California has generally been unremarkable, partly, no doubt, because it has suffered by comparison with French Burgundy. This comparison is unfortunate and unfair; much French Burgundy is made of wine to which sugar has been added—quite legally in France. This practice, called chaptalization, is not permitted in California. Styles of vinification differ in other ways, too. Thus Pinot Noirs should be judged on intrinsic merit rather than by comparison with the wines of Burgundy.

In addition, Pinot Noir is a finicky grape. It is difficult to grow well, takes poorly to blending, and requires very careful vinification procedures. Thus over the years many poor Pinot Noirs have been made, contributing to the grape's lack of popularity. The fact is that California can produce good Pinot Noirs, especially from grapes grown in the cooler regions such as Monterey County and the Carneros section of Napa Valley.

California Pinot Noirs are generally light rather than heavy and often lack the depth of color expected of a red wine. They mature faster and require shorter aging time in barrels than Cabernet Sauvignons. They need some bottle age, but not many last more than a few years. Good Pinot Noirs are velvety and fruity. Some are so grapey they remind you of a French Beaujolais. The varietal has a berrylike aroma and a lingering softness. As we shall see in chapter 14, an interesting white Pinot Noir is being made.

Zinfandel

Opinions about this wine differ, but to most it is the third great red California varietal. Zinfandel, the most widely cultivated red wine grape, is unique. A true *Vitis vinifera* grape, it is found only in California, and no one knows its origin, though credit is often given to Agoston Haraszthy as its discoverer.

Zinfandel is a robust, unusually dark red wine with a briar and berry-like flavor. Depending on the quality of the grapes, the flavor is more or less intense, but a good Zinfandel is aromatic and spicy. It can be made in either of three styles. Specifically for immediate drinking, Zinfandels are refreshing, light, and sprightly, full of grape flavor. Alternatively, they can be made in a big style, with a high tannin content. These wines are aged in oak and develop great intensity, requiring several years of bottle age. Late harvest Zinfandels are made from rich, overripe grapes. The biggest Zinfandels, requiring at least five years of bottle age, are slightly sweet and very big, frequently with 17 percent alcohol. Aged Zinfandels exhibit many characteristics of aged Cabernet Sauvignons, and all but the lightest wines will last for years.

Barbera

European Barbera is one of Italy's leading grapes, and California Barbera is similar in style to the Piedmontese. The wines are dark, acidic, spicy, and generally undistinguished unless made with care sufficient to repay aging in the bottle. Good Barberas become rich, dense, and aromatic after several years in the bottle, though never subtle.

Petite Sirah

Petite Sirah is also something of a mystery, though it may be related to the chief Rhône valley grape, the Syrah. Certainly, it produces a Rhône-like wine: pungent, dark-colored, tannic, and peppery. Until recently used almost exclusively for blending purposes to give color to other wines such as Pinot Noir, it is now being produced quite successfully as a varietal wine, with the advantage of being relatively inexpensive. It comes in two styles: light and fruity; heavy, dark, and intense.

Gamay Beaujolais

Here confusion reigns. It has recently been determined that this grape is really a Pinot Noir and has nothing to do with the Beaujolais grape, which is the Napa Gamay (*see* below). It produces a light, fresh red wine, almost a rosé, which is best drunk young.

Napa Gamay or Gamay Noir

Napa Gamay (also called Gamay Noir) *is* the grape of French Beaujolais. The confusion between Gamay Beaujolais and Napa Gamay is not yet resolved because both grapes produce similar wines and are often used to make rosés. Both are light red, fruity, and not terribly prepossessing. Both should be drunk young, though the better of the two, Gamay Beaujolais, may also be drunk to advantage for about three years.

Merlot

Merlot is the second red grape of Bordeaux. In California it has often been blended with Cabernet Sauvignon but is increasingly being bottled as a varietal. Merlot makes a soft, fruity wine. Though not tannic, it has plenty of body. Ready to drink as soon as bottled, it usually will fade in a few years.

To this list of red wine grapes, one could add others. Carignane (a heavy-bearing grape that produces a light-colored red wine much used for blending, jug wines, and rosés), Ruby Cabernet (a fruity cross of Cabernet Sauvignon and Carignane invented by the University of California to fill the need for a high-yielding grape of some quality that will grow in hot sections of the state), and Charbono (a dark, tannic, chewy, simple wine) are chief among them. Now that we have introduced the principle reds, we turn to the whites.

WHITE VINIFERA WINES

Chardonnay

Often incorrectly called Pinot Chardonnay, Chardonnay is to white wine what Cabernet Sauvignon is to red; given the current enthusiasm for white wine, more so. Chardonnay is France's great white wine grape, the main white grape of Burgundy and one of the chief grapes of Champagne. Its cultivation in California has recently reached a new peak, in terms of both quality and quantity. No better wines are being made in the United States than the best Chardonnays.

Chardonnays range in color from very pale to almost gold. Young, inexpensive Chardonnays, which are usually blends, see little or no wood age, and they are fruity and crisp at their best. Quality Chardonnays, which are usually not blended, are big (with alcohol levels reaching 14 percent), mouth-filling wines, often with a buttery or fresh fruit flavor. These fine wines are aged in French or American oak barrels, sometimes for as long as a year. For a while it seemed that too much oak was inconceivable to U.S. winemakers, but today several styles of quality Chardonnays are produced. These range from heavily oaked wines, to less dominantly oaked wines, to those in which fruit and elegance are stressed.

Johannisberg, or White, Riesling

Johannisberg Riesling is the great grape of Germany and Alsace. The wine is fruity; the aroma, flowery; the combination, at its best, makes for a delicate, flavorful, pale-colored wine. California Rieslings generally exhibit less finesse than German Rieslings because the grapes produced in the warmer California climate develop less acid (needed to balance the natural sugar in the grapes) than those in the cooler and more austere environments of the Rhine and Moselle rivers. In consequence, California Rieslings often seem a little flat.

As a result of the development of new vinification procedures such as cold fermentation, which allows wines to retain much of their fruit, Rieslings are steadily improving. Moreover, a whole new area is opening up with the production of late harvest—that is, sweet—Rieslings. (These are discussed in detail in chapter 14.) The problem of balance in Rieslings is always there—acid readings are usually on the low side—but as a category this varietal is being developed very well.

Emerald Riesling

It is important to remember that *only* Johannisberg Riesling is a true Riesling. Emerald Riesling is a cross of Riesling and Muscadelle —courtesy again of the University of California. Designed to flourish in hot climes, it produces a fresh, simple, pale-colored wine of no special character.

Grey Riesling

Emerald Riesling can lay some claim to the name Riesling; Grey Riesling can claim no such distinction. It produces a tolerable white wine, also of no special quality.

Sylvaner

Sylvaner is often marketed as Riesling, though it is nothing of the sort. Because of the confusion regarding Riesling, California growers who produce the real thing almost always label it *Johannisberg Riesling*; one does well to watch for the qualifier. Sylvaner produces a plain, straightforward wine, bottled both sweet and dry.

Chenin Blanc

This grape, incorrectly called White Pinot or Pineau de la Loire, is the third major white wine grape after Chardonnay and Johannisberg Riesling. Its wines are sharp and full, usually with little color, rather like the wines of the middle Loire also made from Chenin Blanc. Chenin Blanc is made either sweet or dry. The sweet version is soft and lushly fruity. The dry version is more crisp but still retains a fair amount of fruit. The dry version often receives oak aging, which offsets the fruit of the varietal.

Sauvignon Blanc or Fumé Blanc

Both these wines are made from the same grape. Fumé Blancs are usually dry; Sauvignon Blancs are usually sweetish; but there are no rules. The varietal has an obvious herbaceous scent and taste sometimes likened to the scent of new-mown grass. Some people find the distinctive Sauvignon Blanc flavor unpleasant, but it dissipates with bottle age or in oak-aged varietals. A well-made dry Sauvignon Blanc is quite a satisfactory substitute for an expensive Chardonnay.

French Colombard

Like Chenin Blanc, French Colombard is a heavy-yielding grape. It is produced for blending purposes, especially in Chablis and sparkling wines, since it has body but no particularly strong flavor. As a varietal, it is sometimes quite sharp, though fresh and palatable.

Gewürztraminer

The Gewürztraminer of Alsace is a flowery, fruity, spicy white wine of great charm. The varietal in California usually lacks a little Alsatian bite, but the better wines exhibit the same distinctive aroma and quite a bit of the spice. They are perhaps too close in character to California Johannisberg Rieslings, which they often resemble in having too low an acid level.

Sémillon

Sémillon is the grape of the sweet wines of Bordeaux, used in California to produce both sweet and dry wines. Sémillon produces a fuller wine than Sauvignon Blanc, which it resembles, but lacks its individuality. As a sweet wine, Sémillon is reminiscent of a French Sauternes, but the gap between the two is wide.

As with red wines, one could extend the list of whites. Chief among the remaining white wine varieties are Green Hungarian (a popular, refreshing wine of no special character, sometimes slightly sweet) and Pinot Blanc (Chardonnay's poor relation, an adequate, undistinguished wine). Now that we have covered the chief varieties, we may move on to the lesser Labruscas and French hybrids.

Before we do, however, we should note that some *Vitis vinifera* grapes, particularly such whites as Chardonnay and Johannisberg Riesling, are being grown with marked success outside California, in Washington, Oregon, and even beyond the Rockies. We will consider varietals produced at wineries in such states as Michigan, New York, and elsewhere. For the moment it is important to remember that one may not rely on the simple equation: California (and the West in general) equals *Vitis vinifera*; east of the Rockies equals *Vitis labrusca* and French hybrids. Vinifera grapes are increasingly cultivated outside the West.

THE LABRUSCAS

When one turns to the non-Vinifera grapes, the task of describing and distinguishing becomes both easier and more difficult. On the one hand, the relatively few non-Vinifera wines produced as varietals are made in relatively small quantities. On the other hand, partly because they are less often encountered and thus harder to fix in one's mind, these wines tend to manifest fewer differences in character.

The native Labrusca grape, with its foxy flavor—a term one can associate with by recalling the flavor of grape jelly—is most often used as a component in a blended wine. Undiluted Labrusca flavor is simply too intense and acidic to appeal to any but a small minority of palates, not a very enticing market; a lack recognized, as we shall see, by the U.S. government in 1978.

Eastern growers solve this problem by blending. New York State law, for example, allows growers to call their products New York State wines as long as no more than 25 percent of the contents come from non-New York State vineyards. That 25 percent, however, may come from anywhere, and most of the allowance is filled with California Vinifera wines.

If the nature of the eastern grape means that few are bottled as varietals, the names of the chief Labruscas are worth listing.

First, in quantity if not quality, is *Concord*, which produces a heavy crop suitable for making into grape juice, grape drink, and grape jelly. Much is used for wine, red and white, and most sweet kosher wines are made from Concord grapes. Its Labrusca flavor is marked.

Catawba, Nicholas Longworth's joy, produces a sweet white and rosé wine. Its Labrusca flavor character is muted, and the white version is quite palatable.

Niagara, resembling Concord in its foxiness, is made into a sweet or dry white.

Delaware is the best of the Labruscas, chiefly because it is the least Labrusca-like. It can be used for red and white wines and is much used for sparkling wines. Since its sugar content is unusually high for a Labrusca, it is particularly successful as a white.

There is nothing to say about *Scupppernong* and the *Muscadines*. Some people like them for what they are: necessarily sweet due to sugaring to make them palatable—very foxy, unique, and an acquired taste.

FRENCH HYBRIDS

Much more important than the Labruscas are the grapes to which they helped give birth: the so-called French hybrids, the Vinifera-Labrusca crosses first introduced to the United States in the 1930s by Philip Wagner.

The combination of the sturdy Labrusca and the classy Vinifera has, in one form or another, given rise to some very interesting and now widely grown vines. There are literally dozens of French hybrids, all with official technical titles such as Seibel 10,878, but the more important have been assigned names and appear increasingly as varietals, especially in the East.

The chief white hybrids are *Aurora Blanc, Seyval Blanc,* and several *Seibels.* The best of these is probably Seyval Blanc, which produces a firm, flavorful, fruity wine. The most commonly encountered white hybrid is Aurora, which produces a soft, pleasant, uncomplicated wine.

The red hybrids are more interesting as a group. *Baco Noir* makes a dark-colored red wine with good body. The strong acid in the wine means that it can develop well in the bottle even though it is a relatively light-bodied wine.

Chelois, a Seibel grape, is closer to its Labrusca roots than Baco Noir, both in body and nose. *Maréchal Foch* makes a pleasant, crisp wine with a fruity bouquet. Somewhat similar is *De Chaunac,* which produces a fuller, bigger wine.

3

SOILS, CLIMATES, AND
MICROCLIMATES

Unfortunately, choosing wine involves more than knowing the qualities of major and minor *Vitis vinifera* varietals and some Labruscas and hybrids, or even which grape wines one likes. Almost everyone who has experienced a wonderful Zinfandel, for example, has said, "Now, that's my wine," bought another bottle of Zinfandel and been bitterly disappointed. There is clearly more to it than knowing about Zinfandel in a general way.

The label says "Zinfandel" in both cases, but the wines can be, and often are, poles apart in quality—partly due to differences in vintages (which we will discuss in chapter 16) and partly to differences in winery winemaking styles (about which one can do nothing, except stay clear of styles one does not like). But the primary reasons for such disparities in quality lie in two factors. One, climate and soil—the subject of this chapter—governs the available natural ingredients going into a bottle of wine. The other, governmental regulations, determines what may be done with raw products, what may be said and what need *not* be said about the contents of the bottle—the subject of chapter 4. The ultimate factor is winemaking skill, which is not quantifiable.

It is possible to produce wine grapes in most of the United States; in fact, wine grapes are grown in about two-thirds of the states of the union. But to grow them well, first the climate must be right and, second, the soil must be right. Soil is less important than climate. How much less important is arguable. In answer to a direct question, Richard Peterson, winemaker at The Monterey Vineyard, said he thought climate was about 80 percent responsible for grape quality, and soil 20 percent. He doesn't know; no one knows for sure; and his guess is as good as any. What everyone knows is that both have to be right.

SOIL

Correct vinegrowing soil suits virtually no other crop. Rich soils make vines lazy, just as excessive sunshine makes grapes fat and characterless.

A perfect example of this truism is the flinty soil of Chablis in France and that of Monterey County in California. Well to the south of traditional quality areas such as Napa and Sonoma, Monterey County is one of the most recently developed premium California grapegrowing areas. It is instructive to note that the best grapes in Monterey County are being grown on wasteland—land of such marginal value to producers of other crops, who have long farmed richer parts of the county, that most of it remained uncultivated until first planted by winegrowers.

The soil that Monterey County grapegrowers use is sandy, granitic, and porous, requiring much irrigation. Testimony to its value as a winegrowing soil is the fact that such large firms as Mirassou, Wente Brothers, Almadén, and Paul Masson have established substantial acreage there.

In Monterey County the vines have to "work," sending their roots deep down into the soil. The same can be said of the vines in every premium wine-producing region in the world. The best vines are by nature poor bearers; their crop will reach top quality only when their natural stinginess is tested by the poor soils in which they grow. This is why the fertile San Joaquin Valley produces wine grapes less valuable than those produced on the coast.

The importance of this rule can be demonstrated by comparing the quality of the wine produced in these ideal conditions with the crops produced by the heavy-bearing Concord and Thompson Seedless vines. It is not accidental that these two grapes are used for every purpose, only one of which is making wine. The wines they make are fat, flabby, and sugary, fit only for blending in the cheapest wines.

CLIMATE

Needless to say, it is not sufficient to find suitable soils, suitably drained, to grow grapes—especially premium wine grapes. The right climate is also essential.

The worst European wine probably comes not from Europe but from Algeria. Along the Mediterranean shore of North Africa grapes grow in abundance in the hot sun. The wines produced from them are heavily alcoholic, dark-colored, dense, and—unless blended with lighter wines—virtually undrinkable. Huge quantities of such wines are produced and shipped to France—where, after being blended, they become a chief component of the ordinary French citizen's *vin ordinaire*, a most unappealing wine at best.

Much of the wine produced in southern France, southern Italy, and Spain is little, if any, better than the Algerian wine for the same reason: A strong, hot sun is more than quality grapes can stand.

Conversely, good German wines are valued because, being grown at latitudes that mark the northernmost limit at which wine grapes will ripen, they are produced in comparatively small quantities often after a season of barely sufficient sunshine.

Too much sun is just as detrimental to quality as too rich a soil: the cooler the climate (though it cannot be *too* cool), the better the grapes produced. The trouble with this rule of thumb is that while one can know the specific composition of a particular soil, one can never exactly predict the weather in a particular season. Some years the weather plays nasty tricks on you. There is always the possibility it will remain too cool or too hot, that you will experience an especially late frost or untimely rain. For example, on March 31, 1976, when a severe frost struck much of France, growers in affected areas lost up to 75 percent of their crop.

The effect of weather and soil on grape quality means that it is virtually useless to talk about California wine, French wine, or any other broadly defined wine. As we shall see in the next chapter, broad categorizations are invariably the mark of wines inferior to those less broadly denominated.

What this means is that the consumers who care about what they drink face no alternative but to familiarize themselves with a little of California's meteorological geography.

California is held to have five growing regions. This division is based on a classification developed by the University of California at Davis. The essential element in this classification is the *degree-day*, a measurement based on the amount of time a particular geographical location experiences temperatures over 50 degrees Fahrenheit between April 1 and October 31. The dates mark the limits of the growing season; the temperature marks the point above which plant growth occurs.

The system works like this: If the temperature at a particular spot ranges from 50 to 84 degrees on a certain day, the mean temperature for the day is 67 degrees and the daily total in degree-days is 17 (67-50). This figure summed for the total in degree-days is 17 (67-50). This figure summed for the full April 1-October 31 period is the degree-day figure for that spot.

The enologists at Davis who invented the system have developed a degree-day table that is now fully accepted.

California Growing Regions

2,500 degree-days or less	Region I
2,501-3,000 degree-days	Region II
3,001-3,500 degree-days	Region III
3,501-4,000 degree-days	Region IV
more than 4,000 degree-days	Region V

A glance at Map 1 shows readily that the best growing areas, Region I and II, are the smallest and are located nearest to the cooling coast. The two regions virtually coincide, I being rather like the inner of two concentric circles. In fact, all the most famous growing areas, as one would expect, can be categorized that way: Napa, Sonoma, Mendocino, Santa Clara, Santa Barbara, and Monterey Counties.

For purposes of comparison, and to underline the importance of the role climate plays in growing grapes, it is worth reviewing the

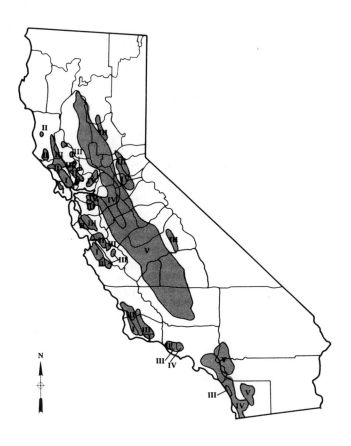

Map 1.   California Growing Regions

major grape varieties in terms of the recommendations Davis makes
regarding their cultivation. According to Davis, the grape varieties
listed below do best in the regions applied.

Region I: Chenin Blanc, Pinot Noir

Region I & II: Cabernet Sauvignon, Chardonnay, Gamay Beaujo-
    lais, Johannisberg Riesling, Napa Gamay

Region II: Grenache, Petite Sirah

Region II & III: Sauvignon Blanc, Sémillon

Region III & IV: Barbera, French Colombard, Ruby Cabernet,
    Emerald Riesling

We began this chapter with the hypothetical encounter of two
very different Zinfandels. A hypothetical, but perfectly reasonable,
explanation for the differences between the two wines is that the first
Zinfandel, the favored one, came from Sonoma while the second, the
poor example, came from the San Joaquin Valley. The purchaser
familiar with the essence of this chapter would never wittingly have
bought the second while expecting to renew the experience he or she
had had with the first.

As we will discover in chapter 4, it is not always easy or even
possible to tell exactly the provenance of the contents of any particular bottle of wine from the label. The winemaker need tell the
consumer only so much about what is in the bottle. However, some
winemakers choose to reveal much more than they need. This trend
toward fuller disclosure is a relatively recent development. In some
ways it parallels the commercial exploitation of and in many cases
discovery of the microclimate.

MICROCLIMATES

Europeans have long known that one piece of land will produce
superlative wines while another, beside the first, will produce
markedly inferior ones. This knowledge eventually gave rise to the
importance attached to vineyard designation, especially in Burgundy.

Californians as well have been aware that wines produced by
vines in certain locations manifest a character different from wines
produced from otherwise identical vines planted nearby. Developing consumer awareness and appreciation of these differences is,
however, an expensive and time-consuming practice. With a few
notable exceptions such as Beaulieu and in a very limited way, little
was done until recently to take advantage of individual qualities of
wines produced from grapes that differ from the expected.

Today the study of *microclimates*—small sections of a given
region that manifest characteristics of a different region or give
certain wines a special and unique character—is of major interest to
all winegrowers.

An example of a relatively large microclimate is Carneros, the most southerly and therefore coolest section of the Napa Valley. The wine valleys of California run north and south, and the water of San Francisco Bay cools Napa. Since Louis Martini started planting there in 1952, Carneros has attracted many growers, most of whom also grow grapes elsewhere. Today wineries such as Martini, Beringer, Buena Vista, Beaulieu, Krug, and Mondavi are growing grapes in Carneros, especially Pinot Noir and Chardonnay.

Some growers blend Carneros wines with those of their other vineyards in Napa and elsewhere. Some draw attention to the Carneros location on the label. The point is that what is happening in Carneros in a big way is happening, often in a small way, in every wine-producing section of the country; and the trend, especially among small wineries, is accelerating. Some wineries label their wines by individual vineyard, if not routinely then still in growing numbers. Many label their wines by section, or microclimate, of a particular county.

Chateau St. Jean is a perfect example. In 1975 it produced and marketed seven separate Chardonnays. Of the seven, five were vineyard-designated, one had a Sonoma County label, and one was labeled North Coast Counties.

This kind of detail inevitably increases costs and therefore prices. But practitioners argue that if people are prepared to pay $20 for a bottle of Château Latour, they will pay $20 for a bottle of California wine as good as or better than the Latour, provided they know that the wine in the bottle has the necessary credentials.

Once one gets beyond a certain quality level, comparisons of wines are the stuff of lengthy and opinionated discussions, much beloved by wine fanciers, and ultimately judgments are rather subjective. But the fact remains that (1) the growing sophistication of the consumer is being matched step-by-step by the winemaker; and (2) the consumers familiar with the climate of California are far better equipped to please their palates—not to mention their purses—than the consumers who say, "What I like is a good Zinfandel," and expect to find one each time they visit their neighborhood wine stores.

4

WINEMAKING AND
THE GOVERNMENT

Back in the days when U.S. wine and sweet fortified wine were virtually synonymous, practically all any consumer wanted to know was its alcoholic content. The higher the alcohol, the better the wine.

Although today the alcohol level is still shown, in a time in which table wine reigns supreme, the wine label is called upon to answer many other questions. Now that consumer protection is a public watchword, it is not surprising that the government—in the form of the Bureau of Alcohol, Tobacco, and Firearms (BATF), a Treasury Department division—functions not only to collect the excise taxes levied on all alcoholic products but also to supervise the functioning of the whole wine industry. Among other manifestations, this supervision and control have resulted in the promulgation of regulations dealing with how a wine is made and, especially, what may and may *not* be expressed on a label.

The following discussion may seem excessively technical, but since the wine label provides practically the only way a consumer can assess the contents of a bottle before purchase, a thorough understanding of the relevant regulations is necessary.

To make matters more confusing, on August 23, 1978, BATF announced a new set of regulations regarding wine labeling. Unfortunately, these do not become compulsory until January 1, 1983, though no doubt many wineries will begin to put them into effect earlier. Until the end of 1982, the consumer should be familiar with both sets of regulations, though it would be wise to work under the assumption that the wine in question has been bottled under the old regulations if there is any doubt.

GENERIC WINES

Largely, wine is sold as one of three types: *generic, proprietary*, and *varietal*. When you ask for a glass of Chablis in a restaurant, you will generally be given a glass of nondescript white California wine. As most people know, there is a famous white French wine called Chablis, which comes from a delimited viticultural area, where its production and components are strictly regulated. The purpose of these strictures is to ensure that a drinker of French Chablis will get a specific and distinguishable wine, of some character, each time he orders Chablis.

In the United States, Chablis and thirteen other borrowed wine names—Europeans would probably say purloined—may be used at will by winemakers: Burgundy, Claret, Champagne, Chianti, Hock, Madeira, Malaga, Moselle, Port, Rhine Wine, Sauterne (note the absence of the French final "s"), Sherry, and Tokay. These wine names, called *generic* terms, mean about what the winemakers say they mean: no more and no less.

French Chablis and California Chablis may be similar in taste, but they *need* not resemble each other and most of the time will not. The only tip the label supplies the consumer is the required addition of a geographic qualifier. The label may not merely say *"Chablis"*; it must say *"American Chablis," "Califiornia Chablis," "Sonoma County Chablis,"* or *"3m 3m Chablis."*

Generics are what most people drink: the typical jug wines. Assessment of their quality is reserved to chapter 5. Suffice to say for now that some of them are excellent values while others are a total waste of money. Most fall somewhere between those extremes.

Generics can be vintage-labeled. They can come from selected growing areas. They can be good wines. But their labels tell the consumer only that the winemaker has decided, for example, to call a particular batch of wine "Chablis."

PROPRIETARY WINES

Somewhat on a par with the generics are the *proprietary*, or brand-identified, wines. Perhaps the most famous European brand-name wine is Blue Nun Liebfraumilch. In this case, the producers have gone to great pains and expense to teach consumers to ask for Blue Nun rather than Liebfraumilch, developing brand loyalty.

In the United States, many winemakers have followed the same route, with one difference. European proprietary wines imported into the United States all have identifiable names—Mouton Cadet and Riunite, for example—but in each case the brand name is attached to a particular kind of regulated wine—in this case Bordeaux and Lambrusco, respectively. U.S. regulations do not require such association. Just as Gallo Chablis, a generic, is what Gallo says it is, so Franciscan Sundance and Christian Brothers Chateau La Salle are what Franciscan and Christian Brothers, respectively, say they are. Proprietary names are invented by wineries and attached to what would otherwise be simple generics to give their wines personality and distinction.

Generally, from year to year efforts are made to keep both generics and proprietary wines unchanged by blending and aging. Wine marketing theory maintains that if you are familiar with, for example, Paul Masson Rubion, are pleased with its taste, and can find it easily, you will be inclined to buy it consistently.

Proprietary wine labels, like generic wine labels, say virtually nothing about contents or quality. You try them; you like them or you don't. Except for the fact that wine is a living substance, susceptible to influences outside the winemaker's control, we come as close to a production-line method as one gets in the industry with generics and proprietary wines. This does not mean these wines are necessarily bad (or good); it means that they are largely steady, uninspired products.

VARIETAL WINES

The top of the line is the varietals, wine made from those of the approximately one hundred grape varieties grown in the United States produced in sufficient concentrations that the wine bottle may—not must—be labeled by grape variety name. The bulk of U.S. wine is marketed as generic or proprietary wine. Just as 20 percent of the best French wine production is entitled to an *Appellation D'Origine Contrôlée* (AOC) designation, the best U.S. wines are the varietals.

The chief varietals are discussed in chapter 2. For now, we need only review the varietal labeling regulations. As we shall see, not all Cabernet Sauvignons, Zinfandels, and Chardonnays are equal—a matter that goes *part* way toward explaining differences in quality and cost.

The three major issues to which label regulations address themselves are: (1) component grape proportions, (2) component grape origins, (3) component grape age: varietal content, appellation, and vintage.

Varietal Content

Some grape varieties are more respected than others. Chardonnay and Cabernet Sauvignon are recognized as the best producers of white and red wines, respectively. But in a day when Chardonnay grapes cost over eight hundred dollars a ton while other white wine grapes cost a third of that amount, there is always a temptation to make a white wine of anything but Chardonnay—or with only a little Chardonnay—and then pass off the resulting wine as Chardonnay. After all, if one can produce any sort of wine and call it Chablis, who is to say that one may not do the same and call it Chardonnay, which is better respected and fetches a much higher price?

The answer is that the government says you cannot. Generic titles are limited to the fourteen already listed, none of which is the name of a grape *variety*. If you want to call your wine by a varietal name, you must put into it grapes of that variety in certain specified quantities.

Nowhere does the government say that a wine must be 100 percent composed of the named varietal. Many winemakers believe that blending enables them to produce better wines than they could if they were compelled to produce 100 percent varietal wines. Cabernet Sauvignon is often blended to great advantage with Merlot—a common occurrence in Bordeaux—or with Zinfandel or Carignane. Other winemakers blend a prime varietal with a lesser wine in order to keep their costs down and to sell their wines less expensively.

But the fact remains that blending and stretching may only proceed so far. A wine containing a smaller proportion of the varietal claimed than allowed by law loses its right to the coveted label designation as a varietal.

Under the existing regulations, wine may be given a varietal designation provided that the named varietal comprises 51 percent of the contents. The new regulations, now optional but compulsory as of January 1, 1983, raise the 51 percent level to 75 percent.

The significance of these percentages lies in the obverse. *Old:* 49 percent, or virtually *half* the contents of the bottle, *may* be composed of any kind of grapes and yet the wine may be passed off as a varietal. *New:* the nonvarietal wines may not exceed 25 percent. This is an improvement. Yet one should realize that in the hands of an unscrupulous winemaker a so-called Cabernet Sauvignon can still be a much corrupted wine.

There is an exception to the new 75 percent rule: *Vitis labrusca* grapes, especially the popular Concord, may still be labeled varietally at 51 percent. The reason for this exception—which may, at BATF's option, be extended to such grapes as the Muscadines—is that the foxy Labruscas are unpalatable at a 75 percent concentration.

One new departure for the industry, provided for by the new regulations, is multivarietal labeling. For example, we may see wines labeled Chardonnay-Chenin Blanc. This is allowed provided the precise percentage of each grape variety used is listed on the label and that the total percentages of the components add up to one hundred.

Appellation

As we saw in chapter 3, *where* the grapes are grown is nearly as important as *what kind* of grapes are used.

Chardonnay vines grown in warmer sections of California produce grapes of significantly lower quality, generally, than those grown in cooler sections. Thus a Napa Valley Chardonnay is usually a better wine buy, but costs more, than a Santa Clara County Chardonnay.

Like the regulations governing varietal content, those governing appellations—the geographic and viticultural names that wines may accord themselves—allow blending and flexibility. The flexibility is much greater under the old regulations, which are lax in defining the nature of more specialized areas of origin. They merely state that 75 percent of the grapes in a bottle have to come from the named viticultural area.

A viticultural area is an area with specific geographic and climatic features and with a known viticultural character. Napa Valley, Sonoma County, and the New York Finger Lakes region are examples. The new regulations provide a procedure to define and publicly identify a viticultural area.

The new regulations are more specific, defining percentages more rigorously and categorizing appellations into several types. The wine may be a *United States* wine, a *named state* wine, a wine from *two or more named contiguous states*, a *county* wine, a wine from *two or more named contiguous counties*, or a *viticultural area* wine.

All U.S. wine must be made entirely of U.S.-grown grapes. Multistate and multicounty wines must be composed of grapes grown within the boundaries of the listed states and counties, and the appropriate percentages, showing place of origin, must be listed.

The really important appellations are the county and viticultural ones. Under the old regulations, these are allowed if 75 percent of the grapes used come from within the delimited area. The new regulations lift the level to 85 percent.

Taken in conjunction with new varietal regulations, the new appellation regulations should result in more reliable labeling and improved wines. Under the old regulations, to take an extreme example, it is possible to see a wine labeled "Napa Valley Cabernet Sauvignon" composed thusly:

25% Cabernet Sauvignon from the Central Valley
26% Cabernet Sauvignon from Napa Valley
49% Zinfandel from Napa Valley

This wine is 75 percent Napa Valley grapes and 51 percent Cabernet Sauvignon. It complies with the regulations, but few consumers expecting a Napa Valley Cabernet Sauvignon would be very happy with what they bought.

Under the new regulations, the worst that could happen is the following:

15% Cabernet Sauvignon from the Central Valley
60% Cabernet Sauvignon from Napa Valley
25% Zinfandel from Napa Valley

This wine—now 85 percent from the Napa Valley and 75 percent Cabernet Sauvignon—is a significantly improved wine.

The tables above should answer any questions about the huge quality discrepancies to be found in identically labeled wines. Even under the new regulations, a lazy or greedy winemaker can legitimately label his wines just like a winemaker who has made his wine from one variety grown in a single vineyard in a single year. As usual, the government has backed away from the most stringent forms of labeling requirements, which would require total identification of all grapes and points of origin, on the grounds that such requirements would be too onerous and expensive to comply with, even though clearly the information is known to the winemaker. Thus, even under the new regulations there will be room for sharp practices. *Caveat emptor!*

Vintage

Regulations, both old and new, concern themselves with this area, too. We will discuss in chapter 16 the quality of the vintage—the characteristics of the weather experienced in a single location throughout the year from picking to picking. The California climate has a less severe effect on the quality of wine produced than that of Europe.

Nevertheless, each year *does* differ from those that precede and follow, producing better or worse wines. At the viticultural-area level, especially when wines are produced from grapes grown in a single vineyard, the differences can be considerable.

Under both old and new regulations, a wine may display a vintage date only if 95 percent of the grapes used are grown in the identified vintage year.

The information in this chapter should enable a consumer to choose his wine purchases selectively. However, other terms are used on the labels of some wines. Some will be covered in subsequent chapters, but one, "estate-bottled," should be clearly understood.

What "estate-bottled" *should* mean is that the grapes used to make the wine were grown on the winery's estate, in its own vineyards, near the winery. Ownership of the vineyards near the winery suggests pride and quality; proximity of the vineyards suggests a certain affinity. In fact, the term has been much misused in the past. Few wineries produce all their own grapes; some produce none at all. Yet the term estate-bottled, with its connotation of quality, appears with depressing regularity. Winemakers have argued that they should be allowed to use the term even when their growers are situated far from the winery, because the relationship is so long standing, that to all intents the growers form part of the winery's estate.

Such arguments are specious at best, and the term should be regarded with skepticism. The implied quality may simply not be there. Fortunately, the new regulations take a more stringent view of the matter. By the end of 1982, estate-bottled *will* mean that the winery owns or tightly controls the producing vineyards and that both winery and vineyards lie in one viticultural area.

Finally, wineries *may* supply other useful information on wine labels—often on a back or neck label—to help the consumer identify and assess the contents. More expensive wines are especially likely to provide such information as vineyard source, grape sugar levels at time of picking, and the like. These data are useful for the serious student of wines, but until one is quite familiar with the varieties and producers they do not provide much practical help.

A WORD OF CAUTION

The alert consumer will stand a fair chance of determining in advance the *technical* components of the wine, especially when the new regulations are fully operative. However, one cannot stress too strongly that this whole chapter has been a matter of arithmetic. Other factors being equal, wine made from better constituent parts will be better than wine made from inferior ones, and the label may help one arrive at a satisfactory analysis of those components. But in winemaking, factors are *never* equal. The skill or mistakes of the winemaker, the apportionment of luck in the form of good weather, etc., can never be taken into account by the label. Wine drinkers make the greatest mistake of all if they "drink the label," judging the wine by label or price. They may *choose* a wine that way. The judging is a sensory event, fully divorced from mathematics. Quality must be determined oneself *after* opening the bottle.

5

JUG WINES
Getting the Most for the Least

Something like 80 percent of all wines drunk in the United States are jug wines—wines that used to be defined as those sold in bottles larger than the customary four-fifths-quart size: in gallons (even, nowadays, in gallon boxes), half-gallons, and magnums; in 1.5, 3, and 4 liters under the metric system introduced for all wines bottled after January 1, 1979.

The metric equivalents for the customary nonmetric sizes, which will still be available after January 1, 1979, until stocks are used up, are as follows:

4/5 quart	25.6 oz.
1 quart	32 oz.
1 magnum	51.2 oz.
1 half-gallon	64 oz.
1 gallon	128 oz.
750 milliliters	25.5 oz.
1 liter	33.8 oz.
1.5 liters	50.7 oz.
3 liters	101.4 oz.
4 liters	135.2 oz.

Jug wines used to be only generics or proprietary wines. Such wines are still packaged as jugs. In addition, one must now include in this classification some varietals and some one-fifth-size-only generics. These, despite the fact that they differ from the ōld jug definition, are included in this book under the general rubric: jug wines.

Although we lump all these wines together in one category, they are not by any means the same in style, quality, price, or value. We will try to isolate some differences later in the chapter. The fact is that these wines can be limited to a single category because they exhibit certain similarities, for all their differences.

First, the jug wine business is to the premium wine business as what is beneath the surface of the ocean is to the tip of the iceberg. Writers, connoisseurs, and experts tend to concentrate on the visible (premium wine) section of the industry, and should, because that is where quality is to be found and interesting developments are taking place. However, what most people buy and drink the majority of the time is jug wine, not premium wine.

Second, no one claims that jug wine is superb. Consumers should be happy to find those that are adequate and pleasant. The U.S. wine industry boasts that the jug wine produced for everyday consumption in the United States is far better, on the average, than European *vin ordinaire*. That boast can be accepted as representing truth, so far as it goes. But it does not go very far. To say that U.S. jug wine is better than French "plonk" is only to say that one makes a wine better than an alcoholic, and generally nasty, grape drink. In fact, there are so many poor jug wines, finding the decent ones takes time and effort.

Third, the jug wine business is geared to volume production. The economics of the business dictate that masses of the stuff be produced cheaply and efficiently. The skilled touch of the winemaker is less evident here; at a premium is the brilliant wine technician. It is true that a small winery—Turgeon-Lohr, for example, or the even smaller Chateau St. Jean—produces a sound and pleasant table wine. But while these efforts are welcome, they hardly make a ripple on the surface of the ocean of jug wine turned out by major producers, from E. & J. Gallo on down. Gallo, which produces more than two times as much wine as the next largest producer; the second-ranked winery, United Vintners (Inglenook, Italian Swiss Colony, and several other labels); and the third, Guild, produce about two-thirds of all wine made in California. Jug wines call for quantity production.

Volume production requires a form of commitment quite different from that required for premium wine production. The aim is to produce a wine that the public en masse likes, not the best wine that can be produced within limits publicly proclaimed or privately held.

Finally, jug wines are that category of wine with which BATF labeling regulations are least concerned. The use of generic titling is in no way modified by the new regulations, despite the fact that it is misleading and meaningless. Except for the proprietor's identification, no additional information is now or will be required.

Current winery identification labeling practice is a very lax affair; therefore consumers are often led astray even with careful reading of the label. What is at issue is the use of such terms as "produced and bottled by" and the name of the producer given. If a label says the wine was "produced by" a particular winery, it means that this winery actually made the wine. However, often the label says the wine was "made by," "vinted by," "finished by," or other such phrase. In these cases the wine was probably made by another, unnamed, winery and not by the one listed. By law no clue as to who actually made the wine or where it was made, let alone where the grapes came from, need be provided, though this information would be helpful to educated consumers of wine.

For example, if the label reads that *ABC* Napa Valley winery made the wine, one would expect it to reflect the winery's style and perhaps be composed of Napa Valley grapes. If one knew that it actually came from grapes grown in the Central Valley and was made into wine by a totally different operation, one would assess the bottle in quite a different light.

By 1983 this situation will have been rectified. The new regulations require accurate identification of all wineries involved in the wine's production.

Linked with this improvement is another, which, for obvious reasons, was also opposed by the industry, concerning the practice of masking the identity of the operating winery by means of DBA names. Until January 1, 1983, wineries may list the producer as another entity, because the producer is "doing business as" the shell operation. The reason for this obfuscation is obvious. If you do not like the wines of *XYZ* winery and have no opinion about the wines of *MNO* winery, you might well buy *MNO's wine, though you most certainly would not if you knew that MNO* is a DBA name for *XYZ*.

After the end of 1982, the form-of-address problem will be solved for consumers. The new regulations require the abandonment of the practice of using DBA names and demand accurate statements regarding who has done what to a certain wine. If the named winery has not done it all, a label could read: "Produced at Gilroy, CA, by *JKL* Vineyards and bottled at San Mateo, CA, by *PQR* Winery."

It is a measure of the little help the jug wine label gives the consumer that we have spent so much time on this relatively minor labeling detail. When so little information is offered, one must make the most of what is there.

The winemaking styles of jug wine producers vary immensely, as do the types, percentages, and qualities of the constituent grapes. The only given fact is that wineries try to ensure uniformity in their jugs from one year to another. A person happy with a *DEF* widget will probably buy *DEF* widgets as long as they are available. Should *DEF* suddenly and radically redesign its widget, it may lose its hitherto contented, but now disturbed, customers. Jug producers from Gallo to the smallest allow change, insofar as it is in the winemaker's control, to occur only very gradually.

A perfect example of this rule is the very popular Gallo Hearty Burgundy. As Gallo, in common with the industry at large, has detected a change in wine tastes in the general public toward slightly sweeter wines, it has altered the style of Hearty Burgundy. But because it caters to popular taste, the wine has maintained its popularity, and that is the name of the game.

This emphasis on uniformity can be compromised in many ways, for good or bad. Wine, finally, is not plastic; it is a living thing. Its production cannot be controlled to the ultimate degree; and only in the very biggest operations is control exercised to the ultimate-less-one degree. But enormous efforts *are* still expended. One unfortunate development designed to give technicians greater control over the wine production involves the use of grape concentrate in place of fresh grapes. The deleterious effects are obvious to the taste. Robert Finigan, publisher of *Robert Finigan's Private Guide to Wines*, a newsletter, maintains that wines made from concentrate bear as little resemblance to real wine as reconstituted orange juice bears to fresh-squeezed orange juice. Finigan may be exaggerating, but the sterile quality of many jug wines may indeed be attributable to this practice. The law on concentrates entirely favors wineries that use them, and they, you may be sure, are not saying anything on the subject.

Technicians cannot do without grapes yet. Other things being equal—and they seldom are—jug wines will be better (or worse) if made from better (or worse) grapes, and at least for red jugs better grapes than hitherto were available for use are now being used. Through the middle years of the 1970s California experienced a vineyard-planting boom, which has now largely dissipated, and since the late 1960s, significant numbers of new vineyard acres, planted mostly with premium varietals, have begun to bear.

This has resulted in an overabundance of some varietal types. Premium wines cannot successfully be made from grapes of young vines. Yet those vines still bear, and their grapes are premium varietal grapes, even though they are of a lesser quality than those from more established vines.

In addition, many vineyardists miscalculated, planting heavily red wine grapes. Now much-desired white wine grapes have also been planted, of course, but the demand for white wine is so great there is little additional grape juice to spare. Such is not the case with reds, especially with less popular varietals such as Pinot Noir.

The total overproduction has been absorbed by jug producers. For example, since 1972 much good Pinot Noir has found its way into jugs. In addition, grapes from such young varietals as Cabernet Sauvignon, Zinfandel, and Petite Sirah have become available, as well as from premium varietals planted in less than ideal locations. Gallo is now the largest purchaser of Napa Valley and Monterey County grapes, even though most of its grapes are still grown in the Central Valley. Most jug producers now use substantial quantities of premium varietals in their jugs.

This process works both ways. The current demand for white wines of all grades has put pressure on the supply system. By 1977, according to a study conducted by an industry newsletter, *Impact*, for the first time more white wine than red was being produced in California, and the trend was accelerating. Thus, while red jugs have been reaping the benefit of the overabundance of premium red varietals, white jugs have been cheated of this advantage. This accounts for the uniformly lower quality of white jugs in comparison with red jugs.

Although premium varietals are being used, especially in red jugs, varietal jugs should not necessarily be considered superior to generic and proprietary jugs, many of which are entitled to take a varietal appellation but choose not to.

Equally important is the consideration that producers of varietal jugs always have at least two varietal lines. Sebastiani, for example, has Mountain varietals and varietals distinguished by a regional or viticultural appellation. The Mountain line is the jug line, and

Sebastiani naturally keeps its best grapes for its top-line varietals. The jug varietals of Sebastiani may well be good wines. However, its varietal jug label does not qualify it as automatically superior to generic and proprietary jugs. The varietal jug may be better, and almost certainly will have a more distinctive quality, but each jug must be judged on its own merits without regard to its label.

The whole question of labeling is rampant with conflicting opinions, and since BATF is taking no sides in the matter at the jug level, it is encouraging to see some wineries taking a positive lead. There is a trend among serious winemakers to do away with generic labels and high-sounding but meaningless proprietary names in favor of simple statements.

The pioneers in this respect are wineries such as Fetzer, which calls its admirable jugs Mendocino Premium Red and White Wines; Oakville, purchased in 1978 by Robert Mondavi, which introduced its "Our House" reds and whites; Pedroncelli; and Robert Mondavi itself, with its Red and White Table Wines.

This decision to use honest, unpretentious labels is to be applauded, especially when the wines so named are of decent quality. Several of these producers could give their wines varietal labels, the necessary percentages being there, but have opted instead for straightforwardness. Perhaps this move will one day be thought of as the death knell of generic labeling. That would be progress indeed.

In the meantime, the struggle with the morass of quality and labels daily confronts the wine shopper. Short of listing some generally acceptable wines, which we do at the end of this chapter, we can only identify a few basic guidelines.

Jug wines, especially whites, tend to be made with a trace of sweetness. Jug producers ape popular taste, which favors a slightly sweet finish to the wine. In this case, they reap an added bonus: The residual sugars in the wines help mask the inadequacies of the component grapes. Winegrapes finished quite dry are more likely to exhibit their weaknesses than if finished sweet.

Red jugs made young and grapey, similar to Beaujolais, are usually called Burgundy or Claret. Chiantis are somewhat heavier (as are some Burgundies). The heaviest, usually having been aged a year or so in huge redwood vats, are the Italian-style, Barberone and the like.

As for whites, quantity, in a white wine-drinking world, is a paramount consideration. Wines are finished dry, not often successfully, or more frequently, slightly sweet. Generally, Chablis is the driest, followed by, in increasing order of sweetness, Sauterne, Rhine Wine, and Haut Sauterne.

As long as the winemaker adheres to these divisions, they are worthwhile. But a winery may call a light red wine Chianti or a heavy red, Claret. Chablis may be finished quite sweet.

Even more so than for premium wines, money talks when buying jugs. Within reason you should spend as much as you can afford. You almost certainly will be getting a better wine if you spend more. Do not get carried away, however; as of late 1978, $2.50 to $3.00 would purchase the very best fifth-bottled jug, $5.00 the best magnum, and $5.50 the best half-gallon, and many good buys could be made at less than these prices.

Bearing in mind what has been said about the right of wineries to buy finished wine or grapes from sections of the state having no viticultural connection with their location, you should buy a wine that is or purports to be from a coastal section rather than the hotter sections of California. Coastal jugs are generally drier and better. Central Valley jugs are almost always on the sweet side. Too much can be made of this when you cannot be sure of the origin of the wine and/or grapes, but you must start somewhere in making a selection.

Finally, a word about vintage and age in general. Jugs, even the heavy Italianate reds, are bottled ready to be drunk. Age will not bring them to maturity; rather, it will lead to their breaking down. The older they are, the more likely it is they have passed whatever modest prime they once achieved. Vintage jugs should be drunk as close to the vintage date as possible.

This chapter closes with three lists of jugs: red, white, rosé. No effort has been made to rank them according to quality. Such ranking is subjective at best. The quality of these wines may change overnight, though will probably not. Most of the wines would appear on practically any ranking of California jugs. Some would appear on few other lists; other lists might include wines not included here. These lists do offer a fairly safe series of suggestions.

They do not take into account differences in bottle size or questions of availability. But few of these wines should be difficult to find. When comparing prices, be sure to compare equal volumes of wine—*see* the table at the beginning of this chapter.

Red Jugs
Almadén California Burgundy
Beaulieu California Burgundy
Beringer North Coast Counties Burgundy
Buena Vista California Burgundy
Cambiaso California Petite Sirah
Cresta Blanca Mendocino Zinfandel
Delicato California Burgundy
Dry Creek Sonoma Idlewood Red Wine
Fetzer Lake County Carignane
Fetzer Mendocino Premium Red Wine
Foppiano Northern California Burgundy
Franciscan Vintage Napa Valley Burgundy
Giumarra California Burgundy
Inglenook North Coast Counties Vintage Burgundy
Italian Swiss Colony California Barbera
Kenwood California Vintage Burgundy
Charles Krug Napa Valley Vintage Burgundy
M. LaMont California Zinfandel
Los Hermanos California Gamay Beaujolais
Louis M. Martini California Mountain Red Wine
Mirassou Santa Clara Vintage Burgundy
CK Mondavi California Select Barberone
CK Mondavi California Select Claret
Robert Mondavi California Red Table Wine
Novitiate California Burgundy
Angelo Papagni Vintage California Barbera

Parducci California Vintage Burgundy
J. Pedroncelli Sonoma County Red Wine
San Martin Santa Clara Valley Burgundy
Sebastiani Northern California Burgundy
Sebastiani Northern California Mountain Cabernet Sauvignon
Souverain of Alexander Valley North Coast Burgundy
Sterling Napa Valley Red Table Wine
Winemasters California Cabernet Sauvignon

Bully Hill New York Red Wine
Gold Seal New York Catawba Red
Great Western New York Pleasant Valley Red
Taylor New York Lake Country Red

White Jugs
Almadén California Mountain White Chablis
Beringer North Coast Chenin Blanc
Christian Brothers Select California Chablis
Cresta Blanca California French Colombard
Dry Creek Sonoma Idlewood Vintage White Wine
Fetzer Mendocino Premium White Wine
Gallo California Chenin Blanc
Giumarra California Chablis
Guasti California French Colombard
Heitz Cellars California Chablis
Inglenook North Coast Counties Vintage Chablis
Kenwood California Chablis
Charles Krug Napa Valley Chablis
Liberty School Napa Valley White Wine
Louis M. Martini California Mountain Chablis
Paul Masson California Chablis
Mirassou Monterey-Santa Clara Dry Chablis
CK Mondavi California Select Dry Sauterne
Robert Mondavi California White Table Wine
Parducci Vintage California Chablis
J. Pedroncelli Sonoma County White Wine
Sebastiani Northern California Mountain Pinot Chardonnay
Sonoma Vineyards California French Colombard
Souverain of Alexander Valley North Coast Dry Chenin Blanc
Sterling Napa Valley White Table Wine
Summit California Chablis
Wente Brothers California Chablis
Winemasters California Johannisberg Riesling

Bully Hill New York White Wine
Gold Seal New York Charles Fournier Chablis Nature
Taylor New York Lake Country White
Widmer New York Lake Niagara

Rosé Jugs
Almadén Grenache Rosé
Beaulieu Beaurose
Christian Brothers California Vin Rosé
Inglenook North Coast Counties Vintage Cabernet Rosé

Charles Krug Napa Valley Vin Rosé
Louis M. Martini California Mountain Vin Rosé
Paul Masson California Vin Rosé Sec
Mirassou Monterey-Santa Clara Petite Rosé
Robert Mondavi Napa Valley Gamay Rosé
Angelo Papagni California Madera Rosé
Sebastiani North Coast Counties Vin Rosé
Wente Brothers California Rosé Wente

Gold Seal New York Catawba Pink
Taylor New York Lake Country Pink

6

CALIFORNIA WINERIES
The Central Valleys, Southern California, Santa Barbara, and San Luis Obispo Counties

The California wine industry is startling in its variety. There are grapegrowers who make no wine and those who make wine and sell it to other wineries, "boutique wineries" that make fewer than five thousand cases of wine, and wineries that produce more than one hundred million gallons of wine a year and are so large that they have their own bottle-making factories. California has wineries that ferment and/or age their wines in fifty-gallon French oak barrels, wineries with storage tanks capable of holding one million gallons; Sterling Vineyards and The Monterey Vineyard owned by Coca-Cola of Atlanta; and a dermatologist, David Bruce, whose winery is renowned for quality.

California has more than 350 wineries, some of which are cooperative ventures with several hundred members. Some are minute. To attempt to describe the variety of operations would require a much longer and more detailed book (a few excellent references are listed in the Further Reading section at the end of this book). Here we only touch on *some* in an effort to get a feel for the industry. By the same token, one must realize that the operations left out are not necessarily unimportant; there simply is not room to include every one.

Some comment is offered about the wines produced. But readers should note that no effort has been made to review wines or to list or comment on all the wines produced by any one winery. Some years a winery is much more successful with a particular wine than others. Thus a comment about a particular winery's Chardonnay, for example, does not mean that all that winery's Chardonnays will match the description given. The comments on wines are offered as a means of showing the diversity of wines produced.

THE CENTRAL VALLEYS
SACRAMENTO AND SAN JOAQUIN

The San Joaquin Valley, which runs northwest and southeast from Lodi to Bakersfield, is perhaps the most fertile valley in the world, averaging forty miles in width along its two hundred miles. Nearly half a million acres of this highly irrigated agricultural gold mine are covered with vineyards. This is Region IV and V land, hot, and the grape crops are huge, on a per-acre basis often twice what the yields are closer to the coast. The wines made from them generally lack the intensity and distinctiveness of coast wines.

From the San Joaquin Valley comes more than three-quarters of all wine produced in California, along with much of the agricultural produce of California.

Above Lodi, the real beginning of the valley, lies the Sacramento Valley, where we begin our tour of the central valleys, not because much wine is produced in the Sacramento Valley, but because the San Joaquin wine industry was spawned by its northern neighbor.

Sacramento Valley

This valley dates its wine industry to the Gold Rush days. In fact, Captain John Sutter, the settler on whose land gold first was discovered, was making brandy in Sacramento as early as 1842, when he introduced vines to Sutter County in the gold lands. Sutter County was the site where Thompson Seedless grapes first were grown in the United States, and it was from there that vines were exported to the San Joaquin Valley to provide the backbone of the table grape and wine industries.

Leland Stanford, onetime governor of California and founder of Stanford University, planted several thousand acres of vines near Chico and established a two-million-gallon winery, the largest in the world, in the late nineteenth century. Even when his table wine operation floundered, Stanford remained the largest brandy distiller in the world.

The area maintained its leading winemaking role until Prohibition. In 1920 there were dozens of operating wineries and some forty thousand acres of grapes in cultivation, but by 1933 every winery and almost every acre had disappeared.

As we have seen, the end of Prohibition did not automatically revive the wine industry, and the Sacramento Valley continued to decline. In recent times several thousand acres of grapes have again been planted, and a rash of little wineries, mostly in the Mother Lode country in Amador and El Dorado counties, have opened up.

The most interesting area is the Shenandoah Valley, which has its own appellation in Amador County. As we will see when we look at the wines of Napa and Sonoma, it has been discovered that Zinfandel grapes grown in Amador, which is cooled by an airstream flowing into and out of the Sierra Nevada, have a unique, full-bodied, and very intense character, and Amador County Zinfandel wines are highly regarded. Much Amador County production finds its way to the coast, but not all.

One very old winery, D'Agostini Winery, which dates back to the

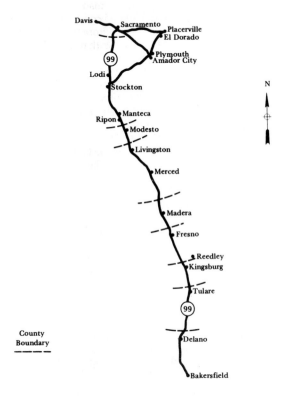

Davis
Sacramento
Placerville
El Dorado
99
Plymouth
Amador City
Lodi
Stockton
Manteca
Ripon
Modesto
Livingston
Merced
Madera
Fresno
Reedley
Kingsburg
Tulare
99
Delano
Bakersfield

N

County
Boundary
— — — —

*Map 2.   Sacramento and San Joaquin Valleys:
Chief Towns and County Lines*

1850s, produces very sound red wines, mostly for local consumption. Another winery, founded in 1973, Montevina, produces some excellent wines, particularly Zinfandels—including a nouveau Zinfandel, called Zinfandel Nuevo, quite like a Nouveau Beaujolais—Sauvignon Blancs, both dry and sweet, and Cabernet Sauvignons.

There are a handful of other small wineries in the region, including Cosumnes River Vineyard and Boeger Winery, and given the estimation being accorded Amador County grapes, one can expect to see others arrive.

San Joaquin Valley

To turn directly from Amador County to Lodi is to move from the flea to the elephant, or at least the elephant's trunk. From the perspective of Lodi and the valley producers, all but the very largest nonvalley producers are so small as to be insignificant. There are small producers in the valley, of course, but they are generally members of a cooperative or they produce for a local market.

Lodi, the center of a separate viticultural section with its own appellation, produces better grapes than the rest of the valley because it is cooler—cool Region IV—than the more southerly parts, and its potential was recognized sooner. As early as 1850 grapes were being cultivated in San Joaquin County not far from Lodi. But Lodi came into its own with the discovery that Flame Tokay grew exceptionally well around the town. Flame Tokay is to California brandy as chocolate is to cake: You can make brandy without using this grape but you will not be happy with the result. Today most brandy produced in the United States originates in Lodi vineyards.

There are more than fifty thousand acres of grapes in San Joaquin County, and though the bulk are Flame Tokay, there are generous plantings of Zinfandel and Carignane and lesser plantings of other varieties.

Much of the vineyards' production is sold to other wineries in the valley and on the coast. But that is the way of the valley. Lodi wineries do the same, buying locally and from great distances.

The chief Lodi operation is Guild—Guild Wineries and Distilleries—the third-largest winemaker in the United States. Guild is a cooperative, started after the repeal of Prohibition by growers who grew desperate as wineries declined to pay what they thought were fair prices for their crops. Today its membership numbers over one thousand, and the winery has a storage capacity in excess of fifty million gallons.

Guild owns a long list of labels, including Cribari, Roma, and Cresta Blanca—the latter operates in Ukiah, in Mendocino County (*see* below)—but its best-known wine is Vino da Tavola, a red proprietary wine distinguished by its red-checked-tablecloth label. This slightly sweet mixture of Zinfandel, Port, and Carignane has been one of the great success stories of the past thirty years.

Since 1974 Guild has had a varietal line of wines under its Winemasters label, with Cabernet Sauvignon and Chenin Blanc being two of its better wines.

The next largest wineries in Lodi are substantially smaller than Guild. East-Side Winery is, like Guild, a cooperative. Unlike Guild, it has always been a rather progressive operation for a cooperative, largely as a result of its founding winemaker, Herman Ehlers. The East-Side Winery, for example, was one of the first to get its growers to plant quality varietals and such Davis-developed special high-temperature grapes as Emerald Riesling and Ruby Cabernet. This farsightedness allowed East-Side to enter the premium wine business as long ago as 1962. Its enthusiasm for quality has been matched by its embrace of new technology, evidenced by installation of stainless steel temperature-controlled tanks far sooner than most other valley wineries.

The results of the effort are to be seen in East-Side's Conti Royale line of varietals—including Cabernet Sauvignon, Zinfandel, Petite Sirah, and Ruby Cabernet—and in its other wines sold under a variety of labels, the chief being Royal Host.

East-Side has a capacity of about five million gallons; Barengo Vineyards has about two million; both date to 1934. Barengo is notable as the first home of the Cesare Mondavi family and as the first producer of Ruby Cabernet, probably its best wine. It still produces for other wineries, such as CK jug wines for C. Mondavi & Sons, but is best known for its May wine, a woodruff-flavored German-style, its wine vinegar, its Zinfandels and Petite Sirahs.

Several other Lodi wineries produce in bulk for such names as Gallo and United Vintners.

Across the county line, in Stanislaus County, is Modesto, home of E. & J. Gallo Winery, the world's largest wine producer. Gallo statistics stagger the mind. It sells over one hundred million gallons a year—over a quarter of all wine, of whatever source, sold in the United States. Gallo has storage capacity for well over two hundred million gallons of wine, including a tank that can hold one million gallons. Gallo's Livingston winery, almost brand-new, is the world's largest. Gallo has its own bottle factory and the world's largest private wine and grape research laboratory. It is the largest producer and/or purchaser of grapes in every part of the state, including the North Coast Counties.

Gallo is also a private company, unwilling to release facts and statistics about its operation. Still run by Ernest and Julio and their families, it was founded on a few thousand dollars of borrowed money in 1933, right after the repeal of Prohibition.

Gallo started to bottle and sell its own wines, rather than sell them in bulk, in 1940. No Gallo wines are great. The aim of Gallo from the beginning has been to supply a quality product for the U.S. consumer for everyday use at everyday prices. It is thus unfair to say that Gallo wines are not fine: they were never intended to be. One can say that, in general, they are what they set out to be. Very few wineries can claim as much. Probably few consumers realize how much Gallo has done, itself and by example, to insure that everyday drinking wine in the United States is superior to that in any other part of the world.

Gallo is production-line oriented. All wines are produced under the most modern conditions—using all-steel, insulated storage tanks, for example—to appeal to popular taste. Gallo's marketing and market research efforts are far more sophisticated and were developed far sooner than its competitors', and this success has helped it identify and shape the market ahead of competitors. It is to this combination that one can credit the success of such wines as Hearty Burgundy, introduced in 1964, such concoctions as Thunderbird, the first flavored wine (1957), and "pop wines" of recent years—Ripple, Spanada, and Boone's Farm Apple Wine. Gallo's list of wines and wine products seems endless.

For years Gallo produced wines in screw-top bottles only, saying the caps kept them fresh. But in 1974 the company produced its first corked varietal wines and soon expects to release oak-aged wines— wines aged in huge, four-thousand-gallon oak tanks. As has been noted, Gallo is extraordinarily sensitive to the consumer. These developments are the surest indication of changes in popular demand and taste.

One of Gallo's best wines is Chenin Blanc. It was the Gallo operation that developed it as a valley varietal. Other varietals are less successful, except for its Sauvignon Blanc, Barbera, and Zinfandel, which can assert modest claims.

Gallo controls the output of cooperatives in Napa and Sonoma; buys huge quantities of grapes in every area, notably in Monterey County; takes the total production of Concord grapes, which it uses for Cold Duck, from a Washington State cooperative; and has fermenting plants and other production plants scattered around the state. But whatever the name—Gallo, Carlo Rossi, Red Mountain, André, etc.—or the point of production, one always knows the producer is Gallo when the origin is listed as Modesto, home base of all Gallo products.

To the north of Modesto, along the road to Stockton, is Franzia Brothers Winery, owned by Coca-Cola Bottling Company of New York since 1973. Franzia, with storage for nearly thirty million gallons, has only recently begun seriously upgrading the quality of its wines, most of which are largely undistinguishable. However, in the past decade it has renovated much of its plant and improved its vineyard acreage with quality varietals. Its French Colombard and Zinfandel may well be indicative of future patterns.

Since Franzia has a number of labels, it is sometimes difficult to identify Franzia wines. The tipoff is the Ripon address. Just as only Gallo wines come from Modesto, and all Gallo wines list the Modesto address, all Franzia wines are listed, whatever the label, as coming from Ripon.

Two other operations in the area deserve to be noted. The first, Delicato Vineyards, is actually in Manteca. Delicato, with a storage capacity of over twelve million gallons, is about one-third the size of Franzia and is an example of a major bulk-wine producer that sells most of its production to other operations. Owned by the Indelicato family, who very sensibly thought the name not quite right for wines, Delicato sells a little wine locally under its own label and is gradually expanding this side of its operation.

The second winery, JFJ Bronco Winery, is situated near Modesto and was founded by members of the Franzia family in 1973. Bronco buys bulk wines from other producers, blends and markets them under its own label as low-priced jug wines.

South of Modesto, the next major stop on this great wine highway is Madera, the home of the United Vintners complex. United

Vintners, Avis to Gallo's Hertz, has had an interesting and checkered history, for part of which it was indeed Number 1.

The real founder of United Vintners was Louis Petri, who returned to the family winery near Escalon, just south of Ripon, when Prohibition ended. By the early 1950s, Louis Petri was the leading wine figure in California, having bought out Mission Bell, Tulare, Shewan-Jones, and Italian Swiss Colony wineries, founded the Allied Grape Growers Cooperative (more than fourteen hundred members today), sold them his own company, and became president of the entire operation, now called United Vintners.

For a period, United Vintners was the leading California producer, the innovative marketer. Petri shrank at no challenge. In an effort to undersell the competition in the East, he built a wine tanker and shipped wine in bulk through the Panama Canal to the East Coast, where it was bottled and sold more cheaply than the competition's.

Petri faced constant competition from Gallo, and in the end, although he added a prestigious old Napa winery, Inglenook, to his empire in the middle 1960s, he lost the war. Gallo surged ahead with its carefully produced wines and impeccable marketing strategy, and Petri finally sold out to Heublein, a Connecticut conglomerate.

The fact that United Vintners fell to Number 2 does not mean it has faded to insignificance. Far from it. In fact, it now has storage capacity for more than one hundred million gallons of wine. Gaining on Gallo, it sells about fifty million gallons a year. This rejuvenation is the result of aggressive marketing and promotion of its wines, which appear as Italian Swiss Colony, Petri, Lejon, and dozens of other labels. Its premium label is Inglenook, in Napa, but not all Inglenook wines really deserve that label. The Inglenook Navalle line, for example, consists basically of Central Valley wines. United Vintners does not have a very good record for informing consumers about its wines. The Italian Swiss Colony line, solidly valley-grown, lists as its address: Italian Swiss Colony. It is not widely broadcast that its address is a post office located in the United Vintners plant in Madera. The impression remains that Italian Swiss Colony wines still are made—indeed, a few of them are—in Asti, Sonoma County.

United Vintners, like Gallo, produces a complete range of wines and wine products. Its Inglenook Navalle line of varietals, not to be confused with the real Inglenook wines of Napa Valley, is perhaps its best Central Valley line. The lesser labels, such as Italian Swiss Colony, are sweetish and lacking in character.

Madera County is in the heart of the San Joaquin Valley. There and to the south, Thompson Seedless reigns supreme with well over three hundred thousand acres of the grape in cultivation. All the major producers buy heavily in the Fresno area, which is particularly important to port and sherry producers.

Thus it is fitting that one of the most important port producers, Ficklin Vineyards, is found here. Though Ficklin is small, its reputation is large, both for innovative techniques—picking grapes before they get loaded up with sugar, for example—and for port (see chapter 15).

Another Madera winery with a growing reputation is Papagni

Vineyards, a grower for many years and, since 1973, a winemaker with a strong commitment to quality production techniques. In this three-million-gallon winery, Papagni produces a nice line of wines, including some vintage varietals. Papagni is the first valley producer to age all its reds in small oak barrels. Of special note are its Madera Rosé, Zinfandel, Charbono, sweetish and dry Chenin Blancs, excellent sweet Muscat Alexandria, and very young, fruity Merlot Premier, a wine made like Nouveau Beaujolais for immediate consumption. Papagni offers some of the best values in valley wines and makes better wines than many nonvalley wineries.

There are huge Gallo, Guild, and Franzia operations in Fresno itself, plus a number of other wineries, primarily producers of bulk wines. To the east, closer to the Sierra Nevada, is a ten-million-gallon cooperative, California Growers Winery, which is noted for its brandy and Setrakian label wines—especially Johannisberg Riesling. The winery is situated at Yettem.

At the south end of the San Joaquin Valley is Kern County, where it is very hot—hot Region V. The discovery that harvesting of varietal grapes relatively early in the year—a process that preserves some of the acid needed to balance the high sugars of grapes grown so far south—enabled one to make decent wines led growers to put in substantial acreages of better-quality grapes to supplement the Thompson Seedless vines that had existed for years.

The original plantings resulted in the development of several cooperatives. The chief among these, Bear Mountain Winery—one of the largest operations in the United States, with a capacity of thirty-six million gallons—was acquired in 1978 by a Canadian brewer and winemaker, John Labatt, Ltd. Bear Mountain had been formed when the DiGiorgio operation sold it to a group of growers in 1966. The new ownership changed Bear Mountain's name to LaMont Winery and will continue to market its sturdy line of Region V varietals under its M. LaMont label. Barbera, dry and tannic, Zinfandel, Ruby Cabernet, French Colombard, and Chenin Blanc are some of the more successful ones. Bear Mountain also uses the Mountain Gold and Mountain Peak labels.

Perhaps the most interesting Central Valley winery is the twenty-million-gallon winery of A. Perelli-Minetti & Sons, near Delano. This winery's story starts with the California Wine Association, the premier wine operation in terms of size and strength before Prohibition. During Prohibition, a new company, Fruit Industries, incorporating California winegrowers, was founded in Lodi by Captain Paul Garrett to sell Vine-Glo. In 1950, Fruit Industries again took the name California Wine Growers and established its Eleven Cellars label, since there were eleven member wineries.

One of the eleven was Italian-born Antonio Perelli-Minetti, who had been involved in California wine since 1902, having begun his career with Italian Swiss Colony. Perelli-Minetti went bankrupt in the early twentieth century in an unsuccessful effort to break the old California Wine Association. He eventually settled in Ukiah, in Mendocino. During Prohibition, in marketing a grape concentrate, he announced: "When diluted, do not store in a warm place because it will ferment, which is against the law." This novel campaign brought Perelli-Minetti to the attention of Giuseppe DiGiorgio, who hired the winemaker to make concentrate until Repeal and then wine.

While Perelli-Minetti worked for DiGiorgio, he also developed his own winery, becoming in time one of the eleven cellars of the California Wine Association. Since the other ten gradually departed from the fold, in 1971 Perelli-Minetti became the sole owner of his onetime nemesis and of more than two hundred labels, from Guasti to Eleven Cellars, Ambassador, A. R. Morrow, and Greystone.

Antonio died in 1976, and today A. Perelli-Minetti produces coast varietals under the Fino Eleven Cellars label—Zinfandels, Cabernet Sauvignons, and Gamay Beaujolais among a line of relatively inexpensive wines. Perelli-Minetti also produces varietals made from valley-grown grapes under its Guasti label.

Another major Kern County producer is Giumarra Vineyards, a twelve-million-gallon Bakersfield winery, best known for many years as a producer of table grapes and bulk wines. Giumarra was the first winery in the area to produce vintage-dated varietals, a move made in 1973 for wines under the GV label. Its Burgundy is as good as any produced in California.

The future of the Central Valley is the future of U.S. wine. There is a certain comfort to be taken from what has happened recently. The issue of whether or not premium grapes now being grown in the valley in Region V areas, previously thought to do well only in much cooler sections, should really be grown there is less important than the fact that the effort is being made. While questions must remain over varietals such as Chardonnay and Pinot Noir, there is no doubt that the valley producers of Chenin Blanc, Cabernet Sauvignon, and Zinfandel are helping materially to improve the quality of jug wines in the United States. Significant improvements are in the works when Gallo installs wooden cooperage—huge barrels made of wood—and valley winemakers increasingly buy grapes harvested earlier rather than later—that is, not at the peak of sweetness.

SOUTHERN CALIFORNIA

As we saw in chapter 1, wines were made in southern California long before the industry established itself in the north and certainly long before the wealth of the San Joaquin Valley was discovered. The Franciscans brought the Mission grape with them in the eighteenth century, and Jean-Louis Vignes developed a very successful winemaking business in Los Angeles in the 1830s.

Eventually, southern California winemakers congregated in the Cucamonga district, fifty miles to the east of Los Angeles beneath the San Gabriel Mountains.

Cucamonga

The grapegrowing affinity of Cucamonga, then a virtual desert, was discovered around the turn of the twentieth century by an Italian immigrant, Secondo Guasti. Guasti realized that the desert actually sat on a huge water table. Inspired, he bought eight square miles of land, planted vineyards, built the town named for him, imported workers from Italy, and encouraged others to join him. One fellow grower was the ubiquitous Captain Garrett.

Cucamonga wines became known for their softness and intensity. Wines from this Region IV growing area exhibit a distinctive intensity and benefit from long aging.

By Prohibition, there were more vineyards in San Bernardino County than in Sonoma or Napa. During Prohibition much production was converted to sacramental wine or sold as Vine-Glo by Garrett's Fruit Industries, eventually absorbed by Perelli-Minetti. After Prohibition, the area was overrun by urban sprawl. Ontario International Airport and Ontario Motor Speedway sit amid the remains of many vineyards. Many vineyards that did not succumb to the developer have been destroyed by the effects of smog.

Today, the Cucamonga industry is limited to a handful of companies and only one of significance, Brookside Enterprises, an eight-million-gallon subsidiary of Beatrice Foods of Chicago. Brookside, which produces much of its grapes in the Temecula section of southern California (*see* below) and not in Cucamonga at all, sells its wines through a national tasting-store operation that has expanded far beyond its original California range. Its chief label, used for the varietal line, is Assumption Abbey, a reminder of the sacramental connection to Cucamonga. Those wines that come from Temecula, labeled as having come from Rancho California, should be noted. The Vaché label offers wines of intermediate quality, while its Vins de Biane Frères label is reserved for brandy and fortified wines—especially Angelica, a very sweet blend of brandy and partly fermented grape juice.

Temecula

One of the most interesting new developments in California is the Rancho California operation near Temecula about fifty miles north of San Diego. Rancho California is a planned development rated Region III because of the cool Pacific breezes that blow up through a gap in the mountains and cool the vineyards. Premium grapes such as Cabernet Sauvignon, Sauvignon Blanc, Zinfandel, Chenin Blanc, Grenache, Petite Sirah, and, particularly, Johannisberg Riesling have been planted in some two thousand acres of vineyards.

Brookside owns a large tract of acreage here and expects Rancho California to supply increasing quantities of its grapes as its Cucamonga vineyards die.

The best-known name, however, is that of a relatively recently founded operation, Callaway Vineyard and Winery, established in 1974 by a former president of Burlington Industries, Ely Callaway, who makes a very fine selection of wines and is something of a public relations expert. For a small, two-hundred-thousand-gallon operation, Callaway gets a lot of attention. Fortunately, the attention is deserved, if only because of the pioneering work Callaway is doing in this hitherto unexploited section of the state. Callaway whites are Chenin Blanc, both dry and very sweet (*see* chapter 14), Sauvignon Blanc, and Johannisberg Riesling. Its reds are huge, intense, alcoholic Zinfandels, including a late harvest 1975 wine with a 16.8 percent alcohol reading, Cabernet Sauvignons, big and tannic, and Petite Sirahs. Many Callaway wines are excellent, and none is to be taken lightly. Callaway takes great care in proper wine vinification. Its efforts are being carefully watched as the newest of California districts is put through its paces.

SANTA BARBARA
AND SAN LUIS OBISPO COUNTIES

It is a toss-up as to whether one locates these two sections in the Central Coast or southern California. Geographically, they belong in southern California; viticulturally they look northward. Take your pick.

However classified—on the Davis scale they are Region I and II—like Temecula they present exciting developments. Grapes have been grown in and around Santa Barbara and in San Luis Obispo County for years, and many wineries in the North are accustomed to buying grapes from this region, especially some Santa Clara wineries. Zinfandel is a particular long-term favorite. What is new is the development of significant new plantings of top-quality varietals, especially Cabernet Sauvignon, Pinot Noir, and Chardonnay.

The wines of The Firestone Vineyard in Santa Barbara County and of Hoffman Mountain Ranch Vineyards in San Luis Obispo County are especially noteworthy for what they have accomplished and for what they promise, for themselves and for the area.

The Firestone Vineyard in the Santa Inez Valley is the product of a 1974 partnership between a son of the founder of the tire company and a grandson, A. Brooks Firestone, who operates the winery, and Suntory, the huge Japanese liquor company. The partners have invested heavily in acreage of premium grapes and in a top-rate plant.

Firestone released its first wine in 1975, a barely sweet Rosé of Cabernet Sauvignon made entirely of free-run—that is, unpressed—juice. It was a tremendous success, and as the vineyards have begun to come in, the varietals released show they have been very carefully made. The 1977 release of the first, 1975 major reds, Cabernet Sauvignon, and Pinot Noir, demonstrates that the quality exhibited by the Chardonnay, released a year earlier, was not an accident. The Pinot Noir is particularly exceptional, especially in light of the failure of that varietal in much of California.

Firestone's vineyards seem to attract *Botrytis cinera*, the mold that concentrates the sugars in the grape (*see* chapter 14), and very sweet Rieslings, in addition to regular bottlings, are being produced.

Overall, the seventy thousand cases of wines Firestone eventually expects to produce will probably be welcome, as will those of other producers who find themselves encouraged by the Firestone example.

Firestone's success is mirrored to a large extent by that of Hoffman Mountain Ranch Vineyards in Paso Robles. This should not come as a surprise, since both Hoffman and Firestone employ as a consultant André Tchelistcheff, the most famous viniculturist in California. Tchelistcheff's reputation is such that he will work only for serious winemakers. Both Firestone and the Hoffmans qualify,

N

●Fresno

●King City

Paso Robles
York Mountain ★ ★Estrella Vineyards
★Hoffman Mountain Ranch

●San Luis Obispo

Santa Maria ● ★Rancho Sisquoc ●Bakersfield

★ Firestone

●Santa Barbara

Los Angeles
● ★Brookside

★ Callaway

●San Diego

★ Winery

Map. 3   Southern California Wineries

although the story of the Hoffmans is a little more romantic.

Dr. Stanley Hoffman and his wife made wine in their backyard. In the 1950s they bought a few acres in Thousand Oaks, which a developer later exchanged for the twelve-hundred-acre Paso Robles ranch. The Hoffmans started to plant in 1965, and they made their first wines in 1972. Two sons now work with their mother and father. In time, Hoffman Mountain Ranch expects to produce forty thousand cases a year.

Like Firestone, Hoffman has made an excellent Rosé of Cabernet Sauvignon and in time will have a full line of major varietals: Cabernet Sauvignon, Pinot Noir—something of a specialty with Tchelistcheff—Zinfandel, Chardonnay, Johannisberg Riesling, and Chenin Blanc, sweet and dry. It already markets some of these wines and is one of the few producers of a good varietal Sylvaner, which Hoffman calls Franken Riesling, a bright, fruity, sweet wine.

Hoffman Mountain Ranch and Firestone still have to prove themselves fully. Many is the case of the winery that has started gloriously and fallen on its face. But the prognosis is happy, and the prognosis for the development of the premium acreage of this area for use by local wineries and to be shipped elsewhere is also excellent. This is indeed fortunate since several new wineries are in the process of establishing themselves. Names, such as York Mountain Winery, which dates to 1882 but has seen serious development under new ownership only since 1970, Lawrence Winery, Rancho Sisquoc Winery, Zac Mesa Winery, Estrella River Winery, already winning awards, should soon be familiar to consumers.

7

CALIFORNIA WINERIES
The Central Coast

Above San Luis Obispo County stretches Monterey County, which can now boast the greatest number of acres planted to prime varietal grapes in the state. In one way or another, almost all the wineries to the south and east of San Francisco, in San Mateo, Santa Clara, Santa Cruz, and Alameda counties, look to Monterey County for grapes and the future.

This growing dependence on Monterey County is chiefly explained by the pressure of population on the original acreage. In the Livermore Valley in Alameda County, for example, vineyards have been protected from further encroachment by developers only by special zoning and taxing dispensations categorizing existing vineyards as "green-belt" preserves. As existing vineyards have been built over and demand for wines grown, wineries have been forced to look south, to Monterey.

MONTEREY COUNTY

In 1961, the Salinas Valley in Monterey County offered vineyards that covered about one hundred acres. In 1977, nearly thirty-four thousand acres were planted to winegrapes. Even more significant are the figures pertaining to the types of grapes planted: more than six thousand acres of Cabernet Sauvignon, the single most widely planted varietal; over three thousand acres each of Pinot Noir and of Zinfandel; more than two thousand acres each of Petite Sirah and of Chenin Blanc; nearly two thousand acres each of Johannisberg Riesling and of Chardonnay. Of the total acreage, nearly eight thousand acres are so new that they are still nonbearing.

The reasons for this growth, other than sheer demand, are the climate and the soil. The Salinas Valley is Region I in the north around Soledad and Region III in the south around King City. Region II is to be found in many sections. The soil is sandy and granitic and very deep, and Monterey County is one of few major vinegrowing areas in the world where vines are grown on their own roots. Because the area is so new, it has never been contaminated with phylloxera. All the vineyards require irrigation since the annual rainfall is sparse. In the Region I sections, Gewürztraminer, Johannisberg Riesling, and Pinot Noir—grapes of such cool sections of Europe as Germany, Alsace, and Burgundy—do especially well. The Region II and III sections, father to the south, are marked by the dominance of Cabernet Sauvignon.

Monterey County grapes are somewhat controversial. No one doubts their quality, but they have a distinctive nature. Their taste has been called eucalyptus-like, minty, herbaceous, and vegetative. These terms offer approaches to characterization, but none does full justice to the unique quality of the grapes. In any case, the wines are different: not worse, not better—different.

As we will see, many wineries buy grapes from Monterey County, several have substantial holdings there, and a number of wineries operate there.

The chief is The Monterey Vineyard, now owned by Coca-Cola of Atlanta. The Monterey Vineyard began in 1973 with a very ambitious concept. In a sense it was a cooperative. The owners of nearly ten thousand acres of premium vines bound themselves together to build a huge winery able to produce single-vineyard wines and bulk wines for others, as well as wine under the group Monterey Vineyard label.

Wines began to appear in 1974 under the direction of one of the most skillful and articulate of all California winemakers, Richard Peterson, who went to The Monterey Vineyard from Beaulieu and Gallo. For a number of reasons, chiefly financial, the winery, which has a capacity in excess of two million gallons, found it difficult to hit its stride for several years, never producing more than twenty thousand cases a year. Coca-Cola's acquisition of The Monterey Vineyard—the winery, not the vineyards— seems to have provided the stability and balance the operation needs to really test the mettle of Peterson.

The Monterey Vineyard produces some very interesting white wines. Its Johannisberg Riesling, Gewürztraminer, and Sauvignon Blanc are especially noteworthy. On the red side its Zinfandels, regular and late harvest, and Pinot Noirs should be looked for. It is too early to have much of an opinion about the Cabernet Sauvignon, but the Rosé of Cabernet Sauvignon is very appealing.

Peterson is most interested in *Botrytis cinerea*, and his late harvest wines, Sauvignon Blanc and Riesling, are quite promising (*see* chapter 14).

The Monterey Peninsula Winery, located in Monterey, is a winery only; it buys all its grapes in Monterey County and elsewhere. It is owned and operated by two dentists, one of whom, Roy Thomas, is also the winemaker. The Cabernet Sauvignons are made in a light style, and are thus quickly ready to drink. Monterey Peninsula produces some very interesting Zinfandels, buying in Lodi and Amador County, for example, and offering among other styles a first-rate late harvest wine. Like The Monterey Vineyard, Monterey Peninsula makes a good Gewürztraminer among its line of whites. A specialty is Ruby Cabernet. Under its less prestigious label, Monterey Cellars, it produces a line of generics and lesser varietals.

New wineries are springing up in Monterey County, just as elsewhere in California. The newest is Ventana Vineyards Winery of Soledad. Then there are a number of very small wineries, most of them too small to require comment. One of the smallest, however, cannot be ignored: Chalone Vineyard, the oldest vineyard in Monterey County.

Vines have been planted around Chalone since 1919, but it was only in 1960 that the current owners set about restoring the operation—a particularly difficult task since the winery, located high up near the Pinnacles National Park, is far beyond electric and water lines.

The capacity of Chalone is distressingly low. A few hundred cases of a varietal is thought by the president, John Graff, to be very good production. Ten thousand cases a year is the goal. But the wines are worth searching for. The Chardonnay is allowed to sit on its skins far longer than most California wines, and is big, yellow gold, and fruity, the oak effect of the aging barrels not being allowed to overwhelm the fruit. Not surprisingly, this was one of the wines selected for the Paris tasting of 1976. The extremely rare Pinot Noir is another truly exceptional wine, while the Chenin Blanc is one of the best produced anywhere and is priced accordingly.

SANTA CLARA COUNTY

Santa Clara County used to be heavily planted to winegrapes. In midcentury there were some eight thousand acres of vineyards in the county, though in general the grapes grown were used to make heavy Italian-style wines. This style of wine is still produced in a number of wineries with limited distribution, such as Fortino Winery, Pedrizzetti Winery, and Emilio Guglielmo Winery; the Italian influence is obvious. These are all in the southern section of Santa Clara County, an area with the appellation Gilroy-Hecker Pass.

San Martin Winery is the major winery in the Hecker Pass region of Santa Claara County, roughly halfway between Morgan Hill and Gilroy. Until 1973, San Martin was owned by the Filice family, but in that year it sold out to the Southdown Corporation, a Texas conglomerate. More recently, Southdown sold San Martin to Somerset Wine Company, a subsidiary of Norton Simon. As with the new ownership of The Monterey Vineyard, the new ownership of San Martin, founded in 1892, has led to the stabilization of a venerable but hardly prestigious name, to the development of a new line of wines and of new approaches to winemaking.

Under the Filice family, which still supplies San Martin with many of its grapes, San Martin was known for jugs and other simple wines. In recent years, under the direction of Ed Friedrich, who came from Paul Masson, a great deal of modernization has taken place. In particular, small stainless steel tanks and cold fermentation systems designed to handle small lots of white wine have been installed.

Livermore
Concannon
Pleasanton ★ ★ Wente Bros.
Villa Armando ★
Stony Ridge
ALAMEDA COUNTY

Fremont
★ Weibel
★ Llords & Elwood

- - - - County Boundary
★ Winery

Mountain
Gemello ★ View
Cupertino Turgeon-Lohr
Ridge ★ San Jose
Evergreen
Martin Ray ★ Saratoga ★ Mirassou
★ ★ Mt. Eden ★ Paul Masson
Novitiate ★ ★ Almadén
Los
David Bruce ★ Gatos SANTA 101 ★ Gugglielmo
CLARA Richert ★ Pedrizzetti
COUNTY ★ San Martin
Felton SANTA CRUZ COUNTY Fortino
Gilroy
★ Bargetto
★ Soquel
Santa
Cruz
Hollister

Salinas
★ Almadén
Monterey
SAN BENITO COUNTY
★ Monterey
Peninsula Gonzalez
The
★ Durney Monterey ★
Vineyards Vineyard ★ Chalone
★ Paul Masson
Soledad
Ventana ★
Vineyards 101
MONTEREY Greenfield
COUNTY
King City

N

Map. 4 Central Coast California Wineries

The effects of the new direction are already to be seen. San Martin is now producing an interesting line of varietals with an emphasis on light, fruity, low-alcohol white wines, wines that Friedrich calls *soft.* So far a soft Johannisberg Riesling, a soft Gamay Beaujolais, and a soft Chenin Blanc have been released. The Gamay Beaujolais is not entirely successful, but the other two serve very well.

Other San Martin wines of note are its virtually dry Monterey County Chenin Blanc, a similar Santa Clara-Santa Barbara Johannisberg Riesling with a very rich varietal aroma, and an oddity: Montonico, an Italian dessert wine aged for several years in oak which reaches a wonderfully intense pitch, the only one produced in the United States.

San Martin's emphasis is very definitely placed on white wines, but some of its reds are not to be ignored. Its Amador County Zinfandel, for example, is big and intense, with a strong berrylike quality, and its Petite Sirah is also attractive.

San Martin, with a 2.6 million-gallon capacity, buys grapes from all around the state but shows a marked preference for Monterey, San Luis Obispo, and Santa Barbara grapes. In this combination it is, if not pioneering, showing an unusual commitment, but then it is taking unlikely steps in several directions. For example, it recently has publicized its "commitment": it now lists by percentage and point of origin the components of all wines, including jugs. Other wineries do the same, but not for every wine or as a matter of policy. San Martin's new ideas and approaches mark it as a comer among medium-size wineries.

Farther north, at Evergreen, close to San Jose, lies Mirassou Vineyards, now run by the fifth generation. For four generations since 1854, Mirassou was known for its wines, but only to wineries, since it sold in bulk only. The youngest generation, the fifth, decided to change that and in the late 1960s began to market its own wines.

Mirassou has some three hundred acres of vineyards in Santa Clara surrounding the winery, but the bulk of the grapes are grown in Monterey. In fact, if one winery has committed itself totally to Monterey—besides those developed in the county—it is Mirassou, which is quite evangelical about the wines of Monterey. In addition, Mirassou has pioneered in the introduction of mechanical harvesters and field crushing of grapes.

The growth of Mirassou indicates that the public likes the results. It now has storage capacity for about 2.3 million gallons and makes a full line of wines. The top of the line are the Mirassou Harvest wines—Zinfandel, Pinot Noir, Cabernet Sauvignon, Petite Sirah, Chardonnay. These are all big wines, often late harvest, displaying intense varietal (and Monterey County) character. The Pinot Noir is especially successful, showing a great deal of fruit, another indication that Monterey County will become one of the top producers of this troublesome varietal. The Petite Sirah offers excellent body and a wonderful peppery flavor.

Mirassou wines tend to be light in body and strong in fruit and varietal character. Cases in point are its regular Chardonnays and Cabernet Sauvignons, which are very fruity yet intense, light yet far from ephemeral, or its Gamay Beaujolais, made as a sweet premier—nouveau-style—and as a sweet rosé. One could equally well point to its sparkling wines (*see* chapter 13) or to its Fleuri Blanc, a flowery, sweet wine with a good dose (8 percent) of residual sugar made chiefly from Gewürztraminer. The Mirassou Gewürztraminer varietal is an enjoyable, spicy Monterey County wine.

Far larger than Mirassou are two of the largest premium wineries in California, Almadén Vineyards and Paul Masson Vineyards of Los Gatos and Saratoga, respectively.

There is a great rivalry between these two operations, which is ironic because they share a common genesis and are now approximately the same size, both close to thirty-million-gallon capacity. In 1852, a Frenchman, Etienne Thée, planted a vineyard at Los Gatos and began to make wine. Thée was followed by his son-in-law and he by his son-in-law, Paul Masson, as French as his father-in-law. Though he came from Burgundy, he was most enamored of the idea of making sparkling wines. Masson eventually bought out the interest of his father-in-law and became sole owner of the operation.

The original vineyards became the property of the company that materialized as Almadén in the 1930s. It was bought in 1941 by Louis Benoist, who in 1958 started an ambitious planting program in San Benito County. In 1967 it was bought by National Distillers. In 1972 Almadén became a public corporation, and it is now one of the largest wineries, bigger than many Central Valley producers, owning nearly seven thousand acres of vineyards.

Almadén still has the small Los Gatos vineyards, but the bulk of its growing occurs in San Benito County—which, so far as winemaking and grapegrowing are concerned, is "Almadén County"—and the adjoining Monterey County. It also has a few hundred acres in Livermore Valley.

The chief Almadén wineries are in San Benito County. At Paicines the white wines are made; at La Cienega, straddling the San Andreas Fault line, the reds are made and aged in some forty thousand barrels. When one adds to these enormous plants Almadén's sparkling wine capacity in Los Gatos and its San Joaquin brandy production facility, it is hardly surprising that Almadén produces wines of practically every type.

During the years of rapid expansion and change of ownership, Almadén's quality slipped severely. It was slow installing cold fermentation systems, for example; it was reluctant to introduce vintage dating and the use of appellations of origin. In recent years, however, it has been making up for lost time. In the early 1970s, vintage-dated, estate-bottled wines began to appear, and the winemaster, Klaus Mathes, is producing quite a number of wines worth more than passing note.

The top-of-the-line vintage-dated, appellation-of-origin-designated wines are most agreeable at the prices charged. These wines carry Monterey County, San Benito County, or San Luis Obispo County appellations. In 1978, Almadén took its new program one step further, releasing the first two wines of its newly designated vintage-dated Charles LeFranc Founder's Wines program, a 1976 Chardonnay and a 1976 late-harvest Johannisberg Riesling, both from San Benito County. In time, such wines as Cabernet Sauvignon and Pinot St. George will be added to this new premium line.

Almadén is a strong proponent of rosés, and its Gamay Beaujolais is an especially good value. The latest Johannisberg Rieslings are fresh and fruity. Its Chardonnay sees quite a lot of wood, not necessarily to good purpose. One of the best-made expensive late-harvest Rieslings, and one of the first at a modest cost, was Almadén's 1975 wine. Sauvignon Blanc (sweet) and Blanc Fumé (dry) show what Almadén is capable of when it decides to do things properly; so does the newly released Merlot. Almadén is the first large winery to produce this varietal.

Almadén's line of vintage-dated jug varietals in their distinctive flagon bottles are also interesting. Since it is not set up to produce the very finest wines, its aim is, like Gallo, to produce quality wines within certain price ranges. In this it is succeeding with much greater regularity than in the past. Its whites usually tend to sweetness; Chenin Blanc is especially sweet; and the reds are often too dense, betokening too much time in Almadén's sea of barrels. But all are clean and well made; for example, the Special Selection vintage wines—especially the Pinot Noir—reach a peak consumers accustomed to only the original Almadén will find eye-opening. Almadén's Grenache Rosé was the first rosé made in California, and the standard it set—sweet, supple—has become a benchmark for most that followed, from Sebastiani to M. LaMont.

Since 1942, Paul Masson has been a subsidiary of Joseph Seagram's, the giant distillery. Before that, Paul Masson, Almadén's arch rival, had been dominated by a number of famous Californians.

At the turn of the century, Paul Masson himself concentrated on the production of sparkling wine, planting his famous "vineyard in the sky" and Mountain Winery at Saratoga outside San Jose. Masson was a jovial party-giver, a character, who ran out of steam after Repeal. During Prohibition he had a license to sell prescription sparkling wines and once lost all of the wines to hijackers. In the early 1930s he sold his operation to Martin Ray, another California wine eccentric. Ray sold to Seagram's in 1942, and the new era saw the major expansion of the Masson operation.

Today, under the direction of winemaster Joseph Stillman, Masson is a substantial operation. While it retains its Saratoga presence, its major effort is concentrated on Monterey County, where it first planted in 1960, though it has substantial acreage in the San Joaquin Valley and in the Hecker Pass section of Santa Clara County. Like all major wineries, it buys grapes from all over California.

Paul Masson has a strong line of proprietary wines, such as Rubion (a light red), Baroque (a much heavier red), and Emerald Dry (a light German-style white). And naturally it has a substantial line of sparkling wines, including a very interesting sparkling Riesling. But it came to vintage dating and county or local appellations of origin even later than Almadén. Such tardiness is not necessarily bad. Little useful purpose is served by setting up as a producer of special wines when one is not equipped to do so, having neither proper grapes nor the right equipment.

Although Paul Masson's commitment was more forced upon it by marketing pressure than embraced with fervor, the results are largely encouraging. The new line, named Pinnacles Selection, is comprised of vintage-dated, Monterey County appellation wines. The inaugural wines were a 1975 Johannisberg Riesling and a 1976 Pinot Chardonnay; in 1976 a Gewürztraminer was added to the line, which also includes Johannisberg Riesling sparkling wine. Other varietals, all 100 percent single-varietal wines, are being added to the list, giving Masson entrée into a new area and reinforcing the reputation of Monterey County.

Most other Masson wines, which are neither vintage-dated nor otherwise identified in ways that can be interpreted by the consumer, can with some exceptions—the Zinfandels, the Port (commented on in chapter 15)—be characterized as middle-line Californian: reliable, undistinguished, often on the sweet side, value for money in their price ranges.

The drop from the size of Paul Masson and Almadén to such operations as Mirassou and San Martin is considerable; the drop from San Martin to the next level is precipitous, though well worth taking.

Santa Clara County is home to a number of small operations that, like Chalone in Monterey County, have enormous reputations.

The most famous is Ridge Vineyards, a one-hundred-fifty-thousand-gallon operation close to Saratoga in Cupertino, renowned for its huge, intense red wines, all of which are unfiltered and vintage-dated. Ridge, founded in 1962, is known particularly for its Zinfandels, made from its own grapes and from those bought in Lodi, Amador, Napa, and Sonoma, in very small lots and bottled separately. In any one year, there may be five or six Ridge Zinfandels, including heavy late harvest wines.

Ridge Cabernet Sauvignons—one of which was featured at the Paris tasting—and Petite Sirahs are made in a similar style with grapes bought from the best sections of the North Coast Counties. No Ridge wines should be drunk until they have had several years of bottle age.

Finally, north of San Jose, in Mountain View, is Gemello Winery, which started life in 1934 as a maker of Italian reds for San Francisco city dwellers. Gemello also produces aged Cabernet Sauvignons that are highly regarded, as are its Zinfandels, including a late harvest wine and Barbera. The slightly sweet Chenin Blanc is one of the better wines of its kind.

Just across the line from Santa Clara County in Santa Cruz County, David Bruce makes wines of great power and intensity. David Bruce Winery Chardonnays are huge, oaky wines; one was featured at the Paris tasting. The Cabernet Sauvignons and Zinfandels are made to be as severe as those from Ridge.

Martin Ray, the Peck's Bad Boy of California winemaking until his recent death, sold Paul Masson to Seagram's and retired to Table Mountain, northwest of Saratoga. There he made "Martin Ray Wines": you liked 'em or you didn't. If you did, you had to look hard, pay a lot, and not give the winemaker any flack about them. Some were remarkably good; others were idiosyncratic at best.

Ray lost his vineyards in a lawsuit, and his operation, now called Mount Eden Vineyards, is run on less individual lines. After 1972 he made wines under the Martin Ray Vineyards label, still his way: very expensive, big, and Martin Ray-like. His adopted stepson makes Martin Ray wines today.

Mount Eden wines are not quite so expensive, but they are hardly more plentiful. Its second label, MEV, offers an interesting line of wines at more tolerable prices.

Finally, we should mention briefly two other operations, Novitiate Wines and Turgeon-Lohr Winery. Novitiate is expanding rapidly in Los Gatos and, like Christian Brothers, has a real religious affiliation: In this case it is a Jesuit operation. Novitiate wines are solid and unspectacular; very good value for the money, very professionally made. The relatively inexpensive Cabernet Sauvignon and Pinot Blanc are recommended.

Turgeon-Lohr is a four-hundred-thousand-gallon winery situated in a nonfunctioning brewery in the heart of San Jose. At the moment the operation is quite small, but it has substantial acreage in Monterey County and an excellent winemaster in Peter Stern. One can expect to see its well-made wines, sold under the J. Lohr label, in wider distribution.

Other names that should not be ignored are Bargetto's Santa Cruz Winery, founded in 1933 in Santa Cruz County, which makes a very effective Barbera and an unusual dry Muscat; and Felton-Empire Vineyards, a tiny operation in Santa Cruz County, which has minuscule distribution. Its botrytised Johannisberg Rieslings are renowned. But we must move on to another section relying heavily on Monterey County, the Livermore Valley.

ALAMEDA COUNTY

Down the center of Alameda County runs a famous California appellation, the Livermore Valley, a flat basin exhibiting poor, stony soil. One can reach the Bay Area in about an hour from Livermore, the home of Wente Brothers and Concannon, and that feature has caused an abundance of construction and a major reduction in vineyard acreage.

Almadén has a few hundred acres here, as do Concannon and Wente Brothers, but the total land in production is far smaller than it used to be.

The major Livermore name is Wente Brothers, a 2.6-million-gallon operation. The winery was founded by a German, Carl Heinrich Wente, in 1883. Wente learned winemaking from Charles Krug in Napa and moved to Livermore. His sons, the brothers of Wente Brothers, expanded the winery, concentrating on white wine.

At the suggestion of Frank Schoonmaker, a prominent importer with a major interest in European wines, Wente Brothers was the first winery to assign varietal names to its wines, making a significant effect on its wines and the wine industry in general. Wente, one of the first to see the potential of Monterey County, planted there in 1963, especially in the Arroyo Seco section, which has its own appellation.

Wente is now run by two grandsons of the brothers, but not much has changed in the operation. Wente has always been in the forefront of technological development and has always been slow to change its approach to winemaking. What it does it tends to do very well. Thanks largely to Herman Wente, who died in 1961 and is acknowledged to have been one of the great California winemakers, the wines are clean and made with care.

Herman Wente "invented" Sauvignon Blanc, and Wente's dry Livermore Sauvignon Blanc remains a first-rate example of the varietal, quite distinctive in its herbaceousness and much more like a French Graves than most Sauvignon Blancs. Wente has also been successful with Gewürztraminer, Pinot Blanc, Sémillon, Grey Riesling, and Johannisberg Riesling. It was one of the first to bottle a late harvest wine—*see* chapter 14.

Wente's Le Blanc de Blancs—a blend of Ugni Blanc, a little-known grape variety, and Chenin Blanc—is fresh, slightly sweet, and very popular. Its Chardonnay was until the early 1960s almost the only Chardonnay available and is a good example of a very fruity Chardonnay, virtually untouched by wood. Eighty-five percent of Wente's production is in white wines, but it makes some interesting light, fruity reds, seeing little wood. The most successful red is the Pinot Noir from Monterey and the sprightly Gamay Beaujolais, a refreshing combination of Monterey and Livermore grapes.

Concannon Vineyard is totally Livermore-based, though it buys some grapes outside the valley. At half-a-million-gallon capacity, it is a smaller winery than its neighbor, Wente Brothers. Concannon, founded by an Irish adventurer in 1883, has always had strong ties to the church, a relationship that served it well during Prohibition.

Concannon makes light whites and is known for its soft Sauvignon Blancs, a far cry from Wente's dry, assertive wines, Chenin Blancs, and Johannisberg Rieslings. In more recent years, a taste has developed for Livermore reds, which Concannon has always produced though without much recognition in the past. Concannon was one of the first to produce Petite Sirah as a varietal. It also now markets interesting Livermore Cabernet Sauvignons and Zinfandels, including a fine rosé of Zinfandel from Amador County—all softer and fruitier than most coast producers' wines.

One of two wineries in nearby Pleasanton is Stony Ridge Winery, the latest owner of vineyards that also date back to the 1880s. The newest incarnation is a venture started in 1975 that makes use of Livermore Valley and Monterey County grapes. Although it is too soon to tell how well this venture will do, it has started well, judging by its slightly sweet, fruity Monterey County Chenin Blanc.

One of the most famous Alameda names is Weibel Champagne Cellars, a sparkling wine producer founded in 1939 by a Swiss. Since 1945, it has cultivated the Mission San Jose holdings once planted by Leland Stanford. Weibel sparkling wines used to be very well regarded but are now less so. Moreover, Weibel has not really decided whether to become a Mendocino operation—it has a large facility in Ukiah (*see* below)—or to remain at Mission San Jose, which is now part of Fremont. For the moment it chiefly produces sparkling wines for other labels, and its own line lacks definition.

Weibel is something of an oddity. Another is neighboring Llords & Elwood Winery, which dates to 1955. In that year, a successful southern California wine merchant, J. H. Elwood, encouraged by Rudolf Weibel, established a winery in Mission San Jose next door to the Weibel winery.

At first Llords & Elwood produced fortified wines—Port and Sherry—but in 1961 Elwood sold his wine stores and introduced a line of table wines. Later, sparkling wines were added. The death of

Elwood, in 1974, put a question mark against the winery, but Elwood's widow and son now seem set to carry on the line, having purchased vineyards in Napa and decided to move the entire operation there.

Another Alameda oddity is the second Pleasanton winery, Villa Armando Winery, a company that uses mostly San Joaquin grapes to make Italian-style wines to sell in New York, where the owner lives. Villa Armando is beginning to market a line of California table wines in addition to such wines as its Orobianco and Rubinello. But priorities are clearly established in favor of its traditional market.

8

CALIFORNIA WINERIES
Sonoma and Mendocino Counties

Sonoma County, more than any other section of California, is a textbook example of what has happened to the winemaking business in the state since 1960. In 1960 it was known primarily as the producer of bulk and jug wines. As one of the two best-known growing regions, it could exhibit only about ten thousand acres of winegrapes, many of which were not particularly fine. Today there are more than twenty thousand acres, many planted to the best varietal grapes. More than fifty wineries operate in Sonoma, and thirty have opened since 1970. Many bulk-wine producers have switched to their own labels. Huge corporations have stepped in and, on occasion, left again as soon as possible. Tiny winemaking operations dedicated to very high standards have sprung up. The turmoil has been incessant, especially in the past ten years. It is hard to know quite what will materialize when the dust settles, but the outlines of California's second most important wine-producing area as it emerges from its metamorphosis are now becoming clear.

It is only recently that Sonoma is coming into its own; after all, at Sonoma Mission the Franciscan fathers first planted grapes in the North Coast Counties, and in Sonoma such characters as General Vallejo and Agoston Haraszthy settled and built up their wine businesses. Moreover, some of the most important wine names in California today—Italian Swiss Colony, Sebastiani, Kornell—were established in Sonoma by or around the turn of the century.

Sonoma's delayed recognition and flowering are attributable to a number of factors. The first is the dominance of neighboring Napa Valley, which developed after Sonoma's industry had begun but quickly overtook the forerunner and has for many years monopolized the premium spot, even though many Napa winemakers grow or buy grapes in Sonoma. Another reason has to do with the failure of the Haraszthy Buena Vista complex as a result of mismanagement and phylloxera. This major setback stunted developments just as Napa was establishing itself. The 1906 San Francisco earthquake caused extensive damage in Sonoma County, likewise inhibiting progress. Finally, Prohibition effectively put an end to real development, though the hardy and established, in many cases, held on.

Unlike Napa, with its well-defined shape, Sonoma County is much bigger and much harder to grasp. There are several growing sections. In the south, centered on the town of Sonoma itself, is the Valley of the Moon—nomenclature courtesy of Jack London—or more properly Sonoma Valley.

The producers recently obtained a viticultural appellation of origin for the section. Other sections of Sonoma County, which itself is an appellation of origin, have also been accorded this definition—among them, Geyserville, Alexander Valley, and Dry Creek. The latter two sections of Sonoma County form two arms of the Russian River Valley complex, another appellation, which is the second major growing section in Sonoma County, stretching from Santa Rosa in the south to Asti in the north.

To say the least, it is hard to think of this variety of territory as a single entity and, therefore, not very surprising that the sections have somewhat different histories and have developed different styles.

Sonoma Valley

The oldest name in the southern section of Sonoma County is that of Buena Vista Winery, Count Agoston Haraszthy's domain, which was an enormous operation in the 1870s, with eight thousand acres of vines. In rapid succession, financial reverses, phylloxera, and the earthquake created havoc, leaving the winery easy prey to the effects of Prohibition. In fact, when Frank Bartholomew, then a United Press correspondent, bought some Sonoma land in 1941 as a site for a country home, he had no idea that what he had bought was the old Buena Vista estate, so little was left to show what once stood there.

Bartholomew began the process of restoring the winemaking operation, but in 1968 he sold the winery to a California food and liquor operation, Young's Market Company, retaining the vineyards for himself.

Today, Buena Vista has expanded its acreage in southeastern Sonoma County, where a new winery has been built, and has a capacity of nearly one million gallons. It still buys grapes from Bartholomew as well as other growers.

For a while Buena Vista wines were a mixed bunch, but the new ownership has in recent years put an emphasis on premium wines, particularly Cabernet Sauvignon, Pinot Noir, Zinfandel, Chardonnay, Johannisberg Riesling, and Gewürztraminer. Although the new vines, which are planted in the Carneros region, have not all come in, the Chardonnays tend to be fresh and fruity; the Johannisberg Rieslings and Gewürztraminers are a little pricey but nicely finished.

If Buena Vista can claim to be the pioneer among still-existing wineries, a Sonoma neighbor, Hanzell Vineyards, a winery modeled exactly on Clos de Vougeot in Burgundy, is father of the current flowering of California wines. Hanzell was founded, owned, and operated by James D. Zellerbach, ambassador to Italy and wealthy in his own right. Zellerbach did not care about cost; he cared about wine, and he wanted to make Burgundian wine, or wine as close to Burgundian Pinot Noirs and Chardonnays as he could. Thus he copied Burgundy techniques exactly and thereby made a relevatory discovery.

Before Hanzell's activities in the 1950s no one had thought that the kind of wood used for a barrel had any effect on the wine. Then, in 1957, Hanzell, copying Burgundy, used French oak barrels for its Pinot Noir and Chardonnay. The results were so impressive that everyone realized it was indeed the type of wood used, other things being equal, that gave French wines their complexity and smoothness. Suddenly everyone who could afford them and was interested in making the very best wines was buying French oak barrels from Limousin and Nevers.

Hanzell was left in the wake of the rush. Zellerbach made wine for his own enjoyment, not really for sale. When he died, in 1963, Hanzell wines appeared intermittently for a while. It was not until the winery was bought by an Australian woman with a French husband, Barbara de Brye, that Hanzell settled down. Today the winery makes Pinot Noir and Chardonnay, though both wines often show more oak than fruit, a real problem with Pinot Noirs, and Cabernet Sauvignon.

The major Valley of the Moon operation is Sebastiani Vineyards, founded in 1904 and run by the founder's son, August, and his family. Sebastiani is a fiercely independent operation and one of the most successful—and fastest growing—mid-sized wineries in California, selling close to two million cases of wine a year and having storage for about six million gallons.

Until 1955 Sebastiani was a bulk-wine operation, but in that year Gus Sebastiani established the family label. The new approach saw virtually no change in family traditions of winemaking. The wines were and are blends, for the most part, the reds aged in redwood casks, made to be big and mouth-filling, the whites on the sweet side. It was all one step away from bulk-wine production.

The Sebastiani operation is very sophisticated, however. As consumers began to make different demands, Sebastiani reacted, slowly but, for a winery of its size, with impact. In the late 1960s, vintage dating made its appearance. More and more varietally bottled selections were offered. Stainless steel tanks were introduced and oak barrels purchased. In 1977 the Proprietor's Reserve label was introduced for special wines selected by the family. Most of the reds in the Proprietor's Reserve program are aged six years before they are released, including Angelicas as well as Cabernet Sauvignons and Pinot Noirs. There is even a Proprietor's Reserve Burgundy.

The production of a much more sophisticated line of wines was matched by Sebastiani's 1975 introduction of varietal wines in half-gallons. The success of this measure was instantaneous and extreme, and within a couple of years some 40 percent of Sebastiani's business was in this line. As we saw in the discussion of jug wines (chapter 5), many other wineries have followed suit. Sebastiani wines are not the finest about, but they generally represent very

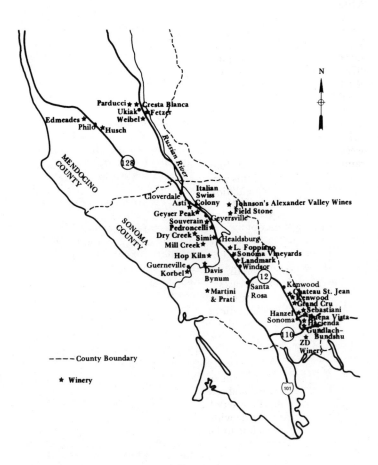

N

Parducci ★ ★ Cresta Blanca
Ukiak ★ ★ Fetzer
★ Weibel

Edmeades ★
Philo ★ Husch

MENDOCINO
COUNTY

128

Russian River

SONOMA
COUNTY

Italian
Swiss
Cloverdale ★ Colony
Asti ★ ★ Johnson's Alexander Valley Wines
Geyser Peak ★ ★ Field Stone
Souverain ★ Geyserville
Pedroncelli ★
Dry Creek ★ Simi ★ Healdsburg
Mill Creek ★ ★ L. Foppiano
Hop Kiln ★ ★ Sonoma Vineyards
Guerneville ★ Landmark
Korbel ★ ★ Davis Windsor
Bynum
12
★ Martini Santa
& Prati Rosa
Kenwood
★ Chateau St. Jean
★ Kenwood
★ Grand Cru
Hanzel ★ ★ Sebastiani
Sonoma ★ ★ Buena Vista
★ Hacienda
12 ★ Gundlach-
Bundshu
ZD
Winery

101

–––– County Boundary

★ Winery

Map. 5   Sonoma and Mendocino Counties

good value for money, and the range of wines is comprehensive.

Barbera has always been a favorite with the Italian Sebastianis, and theirs is big and chewy, the grapes having been picked when very ripe and the wines aged for a lengthy period. Indeed, all the reds are made in this manner. They lose something in subtlety in the process, as they do from being blends, but they have great staying power and almost never dismay by being found thin or acidic. Thus Petite Sirah is added to Pinot Noir because Pinot Noir, in Sebastiani's view, is not a hearty enough wine on its own.

Sebastiani's light reds and rosé of a different nature. Sebastiani's Gamay Beaujolais is a fresh, fruity light red wine. Sebastiani also introduced a Gamay Beaujolais Nouveau, in the French style, in 1972. The Grenache Rosé is a sweet pink wine in the style popularized by Almadén. An unusual rosé is the newly released rosé of Gewürztraminer, Rosa Gewurz Traminer.

Sebastiani's whites are light and are aged for a relatively brief period or for no time at all. The Chardonnays, for example, are fruity and crisp, with virtually no taste of oak. The Chenin Blanc is sweetish and very sippable, and the same can be said for the Gewürztraminer. In contrast, the Johannisberg Riesling, in a day when many sweet versions of this varietal are being made, is dry and aged almost to the point of oxidation. The interesting white Pinot Noirs are discussed in chapter 14.

The three wineries in Sonoma Valley mentioned so far offer unique perspectives on the history and current development of the industry. A fourth, Chateau St. Jean, provides yet another perspective.

Chateau St. Jean is small, with an eventual production capacity of about thirty thousand cases a year. Relatively new to the scene, it first produced wine in leased facilities in 1974 and in its own winery in 1975. But it is symptomatic of a very important development: the desire to produce very good wines in commercially viable quantities. Chateau St. Jean is not a boutique winery, but it is committed, under the leadership of its winemaker, Richard Arrowood, to the careful production that a boutique winery lavishes on its wines.

Something like 80 percent of Chateau St. Jean's production is white wine, the rest red and sparkling. From the beginning, it has produced an outstanding set of Chardonnays, not overladen with oak and impeccably made with a rich, lush fruitiness. Chateau St. Jean's other major claims to fame are its Johannisberg Rieslings, both almost dry and showing varying degrees of sweetness. Few other wineries have achieved the success that Arrowood has had with late harvest Johannisberg Rieslings, which are discussed in chapter 14.

The winery also makes excellent Gewürztraminers, in both almost dry and late harvest, very sweet styles, a fruity Pinot Blanc, an excellent sweet Sauvignon Blanc, and a fine, dry Fumé Blanc. The reds are Cabernet Sauvignon, Zinfandel, and Merlot—less spectacular than the whites but still rewarding.

Chateau St. Jean's very precise winemaking is exemplified by its making many similar wines. In 1975, for example, seven different Chardonnays and five different Johannisberg Rieslings were produced. Is this necessary? Perhaps not, at most levels. But Arrowood argues that the wines of different vineyards and different sections of the county or state differ in their innate qualities and that those differences should be accentuated, or, as far as possible, remain identifiable, rather than be obscured or eliminated by blending. After tasting the 1975 Chardonnays from Belle Terre Vineyards and Robert Young Vineyards side by side—wines picked the same day from vineyards little more than a stone's throw apart and made in the same way—one cannot help but agree that the differences are remarkable.

The wineries following in the footsteps of Buena Vista by undergoing thorough renovation are Gundlach-Bundschu and Kenwood.

Gundlach-Bundschu Winery dates from the 1850s but has been almost moribund for most of this century. The rebuilding began in 1970, undertaken by descendants of the first Bundschu, and the winery reopened in 1973. It is producing very respectable wines in small quantities—with a seventy-five-thousand-gallon capacity—using mostly grapes from the original nineteenth-century vines. The Zinfandels and Gewürztraminers are particularly worth noting, and the Cabernet Sauvignons are soundly made.

Kenwood Vineyards began life in 1906 as the Pagani Winery and functioned as a country winery until bought by members of the Lee family in 1970. The name change betokened other changes: a switch to vintage-dated, varietal wines and a search for new wine sources, one of which was the then little-regarded Mandeville section near Stockton.

The results have been very successful, particularly in reds, which tend to be made soft and fruity rather than heavily oaked and intense. The Cabernet Sauvignons, Zinfandels, Pinot Noirs (especially), Petite Sirahs, Sylvaners, and Gamay Beaujolais are all recommended. The dry Chenin Blanc is a treat, an elegant rendering of a varietal not usually known for subtlety.

Gundlach-Bundschu is not the smallest winery in the Valley of the Moon, by any means. That honor probably falls to ZD Wines, a tiny winery with a capacity of about ten thousand gallons. ZD dates from 1969 and is especially well regarded for its Carneros-grown Pinot Noirs, its oaky Chardonnays, Shenandoah Valley Zinfandels, and Sylvaners. It produces only 100 percent vintage varietals, all aged in fifty-gallon barrels.

Somewhat larger is Grand Cru Vineyards, founded in 1970. Grand Cru is known for its Gewürztraminers, dry and late harvest; botrytis is introduced artificially into the grapes of the latter (see chapter 14). It also makes a variety of Zinfandels, including "white," rosé, late harvest, nouveau, and regular versions.

Finally, one should turn to Hacienda Wine Cellars, established in 1973 by Frank Bartholomew when he sold Buena Vista and now owned by A. Crawford Cooley. Hacienda, which has already doubled in size since its founding, is known for its big Chardonnays, fruity Gewürztraminers, Johannisberg Rieslings, and Pinot Noirs, including a Pinot Noir Blanc.

Russian River

To the north of the Valley of the Moon, above Santa Rosa, is the Russian River section of Sonoma County. In the far north of

Sonoma County, Cloverdale sits beside the generally southward-flowing river, which moves past Geyserville into the Alexander Valley. After many twists, it turns westward, flowing through Healdsburg, at the foot of Dry Creek Valley, and passes on south and west to Guerneville and eventually to the sea.

The course of the river is studded with vineyards and wineries, and we can, at first, do no better than follow it.

South of Cloverdale is Asti, the original home of Italian Swiss Colony. Italian Swiss Agricultural Colony, as it was called originally, was founded as a philanthropic venture to provide work for indigent immigrants from Italy and Switzerland. The first wines were produced in the 1880s; the most famous wine was called Tipo Red. In 1911, philanthropic origins long forgotten, the operation began a migration from owner to owner, until it was bought by Louis Petri and came to its current owner, United Vintners.

The Asti winery is the world's most visited winery, chiefly because it stands beside Route 101, and visitors are all given a show. As a producing winery, however, it chiefly functions to produce wines sold as Inglenook Vineyards wines (*see* below). Of its proud heritage, only Tipo Red remains. As we have seen, United Vintners has even made off with its post office address to Madera in the San Joaquin Valley, thereby successfully confusing one and all.

North of Asti is the Rege Wine Company, a large jug-wine operation catering mostly to the Italian section of San Francisco, Bandiera Wines, and such new ventures as Jade Mountain Winery.

Geyserville is the first town south of Asti, and it is home to two of the most ambitious Sonoma County wineries.

Geyser Peak Winery, a two-million-gallon facility, used to be a family-owned bulk-wine and wine-vinegar producer. But in 1972 the operation was bought by the Joseph Schlitz Brewing Company of Milwaukee, which has funded an enormous expansion and upgrading of both plant and product. The winery is now modernistic in appearance and contains a huge array of cold fermentation tanks, new wood cooperage, and the latest in technology. Development in the plant has been accompanied by new plantings and vineyard acquisitions totaling six hundred acres and by an ambitious grape-purchasing program; for example, much Zinfandel is purchased in Amador County and Cabernet Sauvignon in Santa Barbara County. With such achievements in mind it is hardly surprising to learn that the chief wine man is Al Huntsinger, who supervised the enormous expansion of Almadén in the 1950s and 1960s.

Geyser Peak produces wines under three labels. Inexpensive varietals and jugs are produced as Summit wines. One of the most interesting Summit marketing strategies is the selling of jug wines in plastic-bag-lined cardboard boxes with spigots attached. Summit is not alone in this, but it has promoted the wines most heavily, as befits a subsidiary of a company in an industry such as brewing, in which marketing and promotion are the most important features in any success story. The experiment is being watched carefully: Boxes are cheaper than bottles and are far easier to ship.

The Geyser Peak premium labels are Voltaire and Geyser Peak, though the former is being dropped in favor of exclusive use of the latter. The Limited Bottling program of Geyser Peak offers well-made wines at attractive prices. The Pinot Noirs, Cabernet Sauvignons, and late harvest Rieslings are especially appealing, though all are light and drinkable rather than intense and complex.

To the south of Geyserville is Souverain Cellars, a winery with a short but turbulent history. The winery was founded as Souverain of Alexander Valley, as a kind of tandem operation with the existing Souverain Cellars in Napa. The latter became known as Souverain of Rutherford (*see* below). Both wineries were owned by a Pillsbury Company subsidiary and were another example of the way in which major corporations moved into the wine business in the early 1970s.

In this case the conversion did not take. Pillsbury sold out in 1976, and Souverain of Alexander Valley, now called Souverain Cellars, became the property of a partnership of 179 growers called North Coast Cellars.

The Souverain buildings are handsomely modeled on a Sonoma County feature, the hop kiln, and tours through the new building give visitors one of the best views of winemaking processes. Naturally, in such a newly constructed facility, now presided over by William Bonetti, former winemaker at Charles Krug, everything is of the most up-to-date design. Most interesting is the provision for making wines in very small quantities; that is, for the developing of microclimatic specialties as they are discovered and tested in Sonoma County.

Souverain has a 2.5-million-gallon capacity. Most of its premium wines, which come from Mendocino as well as Sonoma, are free-run, 100 percent varietals. Its premium red and white wines have a North Coast appellation.

The Chenin Blancs are firm and dry, and the Grey Rieslings are far more than the characterless wine this varietal usually makes. The Johannisberg Rieslings are cold fermented, and the fermentation is stopped early, leaving them slightly sweet. The French Colombards are uncommonly flowery, the Chardonnays elegant rather than intense. The reds are perhaps a trifle less satisfactory, with the exceptions of the Gamay Beaujolais—aged in oak casks, which give it more character than most wines made from this grape—and the Pinot Noirs, which are soft, aromatic, and firm bodied. There is also a Pinot Noir Rosé of interest.

J. Pedroncelli Winery, also in Geyserville, dates to 1904, but until the late 1960s it was a well-regarded bulk-wine producer only. Its origins have never been forgotten by the brothers who now run the operation; the wines are sensibly, not spectacularly, made. For example, redwood and not oak cooperage is featured. For that reason they offer some of the best values about, since wineries that have greater pretensions often fail to deliver.

Pedroncelli's woody Cabernet Sauvignons, fruity Pinot Noirs, and spicy Gewürztraminers are especially highly regarded, while its sweet Chenin Blancs and light, crisp Zinfandels, including what may be the best Rosé of Zinfandel, are hardly less appreciated. Its Chardonnays are ready soon, and show, though without complexity, that they are carefully made to exhibit varietal qualities.

Simi Winery of Healdsburg dates to 1876, and it was known for fine wines, though not wines produced under its own label, through the end of World War II. At that time, attention languished, until the winery was bought by Russell Green in 1969. Green is credited with showing that the Alexander Valley was capable of producing first-rate wines. This beginning has propelled Alexander Valley to the forefront as the source of premium grapes in Sonoma County.

Green sold out to a British concern in 1973. Then in 1976 Schieffelin & Company, a New York wine importer, purchased the company.

Simi has a capacity of about three-quarters of a million gallons, all premium wines, and is in the process of increasing its capacity by 50 percent and improving the quality of its plant. Until early 1979, winemaking there was the preserve of the first and one of the few women winemakers in California, MaryAnn Graf, and of Simi's consultant, André Tchelistcheff. Both developed the Alexander Valley appellation and produced some excellent wines. The reds have been especially successful, although Simi's long-term trademark, Carignane, is unfortunately no longer made. The Cabernet Sauvignons are herbaceously rich, even the rosés. The Zinfandels are soft and berry-flavored. Tchelistcheff's specialty, Pinot Noir, has been given much attention. The whites, except for the pale, delicate Chardonnay and the fine Gewürztraminer, have been less memorable.

South of Healdsburg are Foppiano and Sonoma Vineyards. L. Foppiano Wine Company offers none of the visual drama of a Geyser Peak or a Souverain. But appearances are deceiving. The Foppiano story is just as intriguing as those of its smarter-looking competitors.

Foppiano, which dates to 1896, built its reputation on jugs—especially big, heavy red jug wines—and still makes such wines. But behind its unprepossessing facade, the current generation of Foppianos is completely renovating the plant, installing small oak cooperage and all the other paraphernalia of a modern winery, bit by bit and with deliberation.

The results are not all in, but the varietals, the first of which appeared in 1972 and sport a Russian River appellation, show very well. The wines are not refined but are solid and palatable. Petite Sirah lends itself to the Foppiano redwood casks and is produced dark, peppery, and admirable. The Zinfandel is almost elegant rather than intense, in the style of Russian River Zinfandels. The Pinot Noir is likewise austere rather than flowery.

The new developments at Foppiano will undoubtedly result in better whites, lighter, fruitier, and drier. This label bears watching while undergoing its metamorphosis.

Closer to Windsor than to Healdsburg is Sonoma Vineyards, one of the most impressive vineyard and winery operations to be developed in the past few years.

Sonoma Vineyards' history began in 1959 when the current winemaker, Rodney Strong, opened a wine shop in Tiburon. From those modest beginnings, Strong began to lease facilities in Windsor to bottle wine for the carriage trade—wines labeled personally for individual customers. This business is still carried on by Windsor Vineyards, Sonoma Vineyards' second label, but Strong and his associates soon went on to much bigger things.

In the early 1970s, Sonoma Vineyards, in rapid succession, purchased and planted five thousand acres to premium grapes, built a totally new winery of revolutionary design (cross-shaped), went public, saw its stock rise above forty dollars, and found it had a tiger by the tail.

By the mid-1970s, the tiger had gotten away. Sonoma Vineyards stock sank to less than one dollar, and the company fell on hard times. It was saved by an association with Renfield Importers, a New York-based importer of wines.

The saga of Sonoma Vineyards is worth recounting as an example of the kind of strains the industry has faced in the past decade of expansion and acquisition. Just as interesting as the story, however, is the fact that through it all Rod Strong continued to make interesting wines.

Sonoma Vineyards has a capacity of about five million gallons, making it a substantial premium operation. It produces one sparkling wine, but the bulk are vintage-dated, estate-bottled table wines.

Sonoma Vineyards red wines are made soft and fruity, rather than bold and assertive. Its Petite Sirah is drinkable in the extreme, especially in the context of most others available. The Cabernet Sauvignon is quiet but well made. The Gamay Beaujolais is on the sweet side.

Overall, Sonoma whites are better than the reds. The Chardonnays, rich and complex, are consistently successful, and the Johannisberg Rieslings, made in the German style with which Strong has considerable affinity, are clean and light, even the late harvest sweet Rieslings. The sweet Sauvignon Blanc is less satisfactory.

Like Sebastiani, Sonoma Vineyards offers varietals in large jugs, and in this category the French Colombard is notable.

The most westerly of the Russian River wineries is F. Korbel & Brothers, at Guerneville. Korbel, which dates to 1862, is owned by a great sparkling-wine man, Adolf Heck. It is most closely associated with the production of sparkling wines (chapter 13) and brandy (chapter 15), but produced a number of well-respected table wines in the early 1970s. Unfortunately, demand for its sparkling wines and brandies is so great that it is phasing out table wine production.

Between Guerneville and Santa Rosa is the substantial Martini & Prati winery. Martini & Prati is a producer of bulk wines but also offers a line of varietals under the historic Fountain Grove label.

There are a few other substantial wine operations in northern Sonoma. Gallo, for example, takes the entire production of two cooperatives, in Windsor and in Dry Creek Valley, and Cambiaso Winery in Healdsburg produces bulk wines and a line of varietals. But the really interesting developments in the Russian River region are the proliferation of boutique wineries.

Probably the best established is Dry Creek Vineyard to the northwest of Healdsburg. Founded in 1972, it now produces about seventeen thousand cases a year and aims for twenty thousand. Dry Creek's founder, David Stare, has something of the late Martin Ray about him: he knows his own mind and is not afraid to express it. That he, working virtually alone, established Dry Creek Valley as an appellation of origin is a testament to his tenacity and strength of character.

Dry Creek produces only varietal table wines, and since it is a self-proclaimed Médoc château, its wines have a Bordeaux character.

The herbaceousness and elegance of the Cabernet Sauvignons are quite evident. The second Bordeaux red, Merlot, tends to be made on the tannic, rather than on the fruity, side. The Gamay Beaujolais is first rate. The dry Fumé Blanc, closer to a Graves than to a Loire wine, is one of the best Sauvignon Blancs produced. Chenin Blancs, fruity and nearly dry; Zinfandels; slightly sweet Rosés of Cabernet Sauvignon; and elegant, oaky Chardonnays are likewise well respected.

Closer to Healdsburg are Lambert Bridge (a fifty-thousand-gallon winery designed to produce estate-bottled Chardonnay and Cabernet Sauvignon), ten-thousand-gallon A. Rafanelli Winery, and six-thousand-gallon Preston Winery.

Just west of Healdsburg is sixty-thousand-gallon Mill Creek Vineyards, which started producing in 1976. Mill Creek has seventy-five acres of Cabernet Sauvignon, Chardonnay, Pinot Noir, and Merlot, some of which were planted as long ago as 1965. One of its first wines, a Rosé of Cabernet Sauvignon, remains one of its best. The winery is family owned and operated.

To the north, in Geyserville, are ten-thousand-gallon Vina Vista Vineyard and Trentadue Winery, with a one-hundred-thousand-gallon capacity. Trentadue dates to 1969 and is a supplier of grapes to Ridge, among other wineries. Under its own label, Trentadue produces a rather full line of big, tannic wines. Among them are Cabernet Sauvignon, Zinfandel, Petite Sirah, Chardonnay, Sauvignon Blanc, and Chenin Blanc. The most exceptional wine is probably the Grey Riesling.

In addition to Trentadue, Ridge has also purchased Zinfandels in the past from Lytton Springs vineyard, to make one of its big, heavy wines. Those days are gone, however. There is now a Lytton Springs Winery making wine from the vineyard's Zinfandel and Petite Sirah grapes.

The Alexander Valley can boast many large growers and several new wineries. Most of Simi's grapes come from this valley, as well as many of Widmer, a large New York State winery.

Perhaps the most interesting is Field Stone Winery, a beautiful little thirty-thousand-gallon winery built into the hillside. Field Stone is as modern in its tiny way as anyone—more modern, in fact than almost anyone. For example, it uses a special, mobile small-capacity field crusher, which enables grapes to be picked, crushed, and delivered to the fermenting tanks in the shortest possible time. All Field Stone wines are estate-bottled in the truest sense. It grows all its own grapes; they surround the winery—another reason for the short time lapse between picking and fermenting.

The first Field Stone wines were released in 1978: Gewürztraminer, Johannisberg Riesling, Chenin Blanc, and Rosés of Cabernet Sauvignon and Petite Sirah. All were cleanly and carefully made, and the major wines, when released, should be worth searching for.

A year or two younger than Field Stone are Alexander Valley Vineyards and Johnson's Alexander Valley Wines. The former's Chardonnays are big, oaky, and buttery; its Johannisberg Rieslings are light and fruity. Its first Cabernet Sauvignon was released in 1978. The latter operation, which has been growing grapes for others since 1952 and which features, uniquely, a huge pipe organ in the winery, makes very acceptable Pinot Noirs and Pinot Noir Rosés, among other wines.

The oldest winery in the valley is Sausal Winery, which dates to 1973. The Jordan Vineyard, of the same size, one hundred thousand gallons, is the newest. It will produce only Cabernet Sauvignon, but none will be released until 1980, when its first wine, made from grapes of the 1976 vintage, will be four years old.

Bordeaux chateaux must have a special appeal for Sonoma vintners. First, there was Dry Creek. Now there is Jordan, where the investment in plant (the best and the latest), vineyards (two hundred seventy acres), and inventory (no release for four years) bespeaks certainty, ambition, and grand ideas.

In Healdsburg one finds the newly named Clos du Bois, which used to be called Western Eleven Vineyards. Clos du Bois owns a thousand acres of vines in Dry Creek Valley and Alexander Valley and sells most of its production to other wineries. However, a small percentage is marked for its own wines. The best is probably its Pinot Noir.

Between Healdsburg and Guerneville, tucked away up in the hills, is Hop Kiln Winery, another family affair producing almost all its own grapes and making wines in a designated California historical monument: a hop kiln. Some of the vines there date to the nineteenth century. Hop Kiln wines are "natural," unfiltered, well-aged, and available most often only at the winery. Three hundred fifty cases, the amount Hop Kiln produced of 1976 Gamay Beaujolais, is a lot for the winery. The Johannisberg Rieslings, both fermented quite dry and late harvest, are fine examples of what the grape can produce. The Zinfandels and Petite Sirahs from the oldest vineyards are dark, heavy, tannic, and very intense.

Farther down the Russian River is Davis Bynum Winery, which migrated to Sonoma County in 1974 from Albany, east of San Francisco Bay. Bynum grows few of its own grapes but manages to make a very respectable line of varietals with grapes supplied by other Russian River growers. One of its best is Fumé Blanc.

One must stop somewhere, so we will pause briefly at only two more wineries. The first is eighty-thousand-gallon Landmark Vineyards in Windsor. Another family operation, Landmark has produced Cabernet Sauvignon, Chardonnay, and Pinot Noir of distinction.

The second is Swan Vineyards, which is the tiny (five thousand gallons) hobby of a retired pilot, Joseph Swan. The vineyard production is minute, and Swan buys its Zinfandels. But its wines are highly rated, especially Pinot Noir, which is fermented in the Burgundian fashion.

Sonoma County offers the greatest room for development in the North Coast Counties area simply because it has been, until recently, relatively unexploited. Unlike Napa, almost every nook and cranny of which has been examined and explored, Sonoma is almost virgin territory. No one yet knows how its sections will rank in the future. Wines produced from grapes grown in specific sections have not been made for enough years and have not lived long enough for anyone to be sure. Microclimates are still largely unknown or unexamined.

According to David Stare of Dry Creek, "The name Napa on the label is worth at least twenty cents more a bottle than the name Sonoma." That situation is likely to change. The investment in Sonoma, with its Regions I through III climates, is too great for it to be otherwise.

MENDOCINO COUNTY

If Sonoma County has languished in the shadow of Napa for many years, Mendocino has suffered just as much at the hands of Sonoma—possibly more, since Sonoma and Mendocino have been lumped together as one region for years.

That is changing. As in the rest of California, redefinition is occurring in Mendocino, the most northerly of the North Coast Counties, which is now being recognized for what it has to offer: a particular region with its own style of wines.

Although there are over eight thousand acres of vines in Mendocino, there are only six wineries producing wines there. The bulk of the grapes and wines move into Sonoma—where such wineries as Sonoma Vineyards produce wines with Mendocino County appellations—and elsewhere, including the big wineries of San Joaquin.

The few functioning wineries are very different from each other. The four major ones all lie in the Redwood Valley, a Mendocino appellation, and are virtual neighbors in and around the town of Ukiah.

The first in any order is Parducci Wine Cellars, founded in Ukiah in 1931 by Adolph Parducci, who had originally set up his operation in Cloverdale, across the Sonoma County line. Parducci for many years produced bulk wines almost exclusively. But after World War II, the winery began more and more to produce table wines under its own label.

Today, the founder's sons, John and George, produce a large body of Mendocino wines in their father's manner. Parducci wines are aged not in oak but chiefly in seasoned redwood casks, which are so old that they impart no flavor, or virtually none, to the wines. Parducci has gone so far as to release a Cabernet Sauvignon that has not been aged in wood at all. The result is fruity and very young-tasting: an interesting experience.

Parducci is unusual in its techniques, but its red wines are much admired. The Cabernet Sauvignons, Barberas, Zinfandels, Carignanes, Petite Sirahs, Pinot Noirs, and Gamay Beaujolais are especially well liked. It is one of the few to produce a varietal Carignane.

Parducci is especially known for its large reds, strong and honest, usually unfiltered and unfined. But since it has installed all the latest in stainless steel tanks and the other equipment of modern white wine production, its fresh and fruity whites, especially French Colombard, its slightly sweet, strongly flavored Chenin Blanc, and its soft, full Chardonnay are not to be ignored.

The second major Ukiah producer is Fetzer Vineyards, founded in

1968 by Bernard Fetzer, a lumberman—Mendocino is redwood country—and his very large family. Fetzer produces estate-produced and-bottled wines almost exclusively, and, as we saw in chapter 5, its red and white jug wines are very highly recommended. Fetzer's emphasis lies on the reds, which are made in the big, husky style of most Mendocino wines. Particularly successful are Cabernet Sauvignons, Zinfandels, Petite Sirahs, and Pinot Noirs. Several Zinfandels are released each year, often from separate vineyards. Like Parducci it has a popular, but uncommon, Carignane.

Unlike Parducci, Fetzer believes in using wood—both European and especially American—to bring up the wines. The fact that both succeed indicates the width of the spectrum of quality wine production in the United States.

Fetzer whites—with the exception of the Premium White Table Wine, which is mostly Chenin Blanc and Sémillon, and its Dry Sémillon—are less remarkable wines, though the Green Hungarian bears watching for. The winery's second label, Bel Arbres, signals well-made, inexpensive wines.

The third Ukiah winery is Cresta Blanca Winery. Earlier in this book we traced the odyssey of this Livermore Valley winery, which was no more than a shadow when it was sold to Guild of Lodi by Schenley in 1970. Guild reestablished Cresta Blanca as its premium label in Ukiah in 1972, to take the crops of some of its member growers in Mendocino. Finally, it seems, the voyage that began in 1882 has ended—happily for all, since the wines being produced now are perfectly respectable, if not outstanding. Big Mendocino reds, especially Petite Sirahs and Zinfandels, are the most appealing of the now-young winery's production.

The final Ukiah winery is also something of a strange creature. Weibel Champagne Vineyards is an offshoot of the Mission San Jose establishment known primarily for production of sparkling wines for other labels.

Weibel, which produces table wines in Ukiah but seems somewhat undetermined as to its future direction, is hardly a winery by which to judge Mendocino. That role probably falls to two small wineries in the Anderson Valley section of Mendocino: Husch and Edmeades. The Redwood Valley section of Mendocino is part of the Russian River Valley, and for the most part it is Region III, warm, with some Region II vineyard sites. However, in the Novarro River's Anderson Valley, a new appellation, and especially around the town of Philo, it is a very cool Region I. The cold fogs from the Pacific roll up the valley, where Chardonnay, Gewürztraminer, and Pinot Noir are being grown by two tiny family-owned wineries, Husch Vineyards and Edmeades.

Tony Husch and his wife, Gretchen, planted their first vines in 1968 and started making wine in 1971. The big Pinot Noirs and spicy Gewürztraminers are especially noteworthy, as is the Rosé of Pinot Noir, an uncommon wine.

Edmeades is a couple of years younger than Husch, though some of its vines date to 1963. At forty-thousand-gallon capacity, Edmeades is twice as large as Husch, but its spirit is similar. Of its wines, the Cabernet Sauvignons and Zinfandels are the best regarded. Edmeades produced one of the first "white" Zinfandels.

Husch and Edmeades are boutique wineries, in the best sense of the word. Parducci is solidly established, as is Fetzer, which has a capacity of about six hundred thousand gallons. As in Sonoma, more work will undoubtedly be done with microclimates and grapes grown in Mendocino County. Already two new wineries, Dach Vineyards and Novarro Winery, are preparing to open their doors, and there is no question but that Mendocino is soon going to come into its own.

Lake County, to the east of Mendocino County, is only now beginning to be developed. Some Mendocino wineries buy grapes from there, as do those in other parts of the state. Undoubtedly, Lake County will in time come more to the fore, but for the moment one can class its wines with those of Mendocino's Redwood Valley, which they closely resemble.

9

CALIFORNIA WINERIES
The Napa Valley

The appellation Napa Valley is to all intents and purposes synonymous with Napa County, and it produces the polished diamonds that shine amid the North Coast Counties' rough-cut gems. The reason for Napa's preeminence is twofold. First, it has long been known that Napa soils and climate produce winegrapes of distinction. Other sections of California may produce as well, but none produces better for such a range of premium grapes. Second, Napa has a history of premium-wine production that stretches in an unbroken line back to the mid-nineteenth century. During Prohibition and in the depressed period between the end of Prohibition and the end of World War II, the line sagged a little, but progress was continuous nonetheless. In fact, as we shall see, some of the major Napa names surfaced during this bleak interregnum.

Grapegrowing in Napa began in the 1830s, when George Yount, the founder of Yountville, planted Mission grapes. By the end of the century grapevines were to be found from one end of the valley to the other, and already in 1880 Robert Louis Stevenson had in his *Silverado Squatters* indicated that Napa winemakers were experimenting with what today we call microclimates, growing grapes here, then there, making wine, tasting and testing, in a continual effort to produce what Stevenson called their "bottled poetry."

Phylloxera nearly did in Napa , but the growers came back. They even survived Prohibition, though in the early 1960s there were only some ten thousand acres planted to premium grapes. In the next fifteen years, acreage grew to twenty-five thousand acres. More grapes cannot really be grown in Napa today; practically every available square inch of the county has been planted to premium grapes. Lesser-quality vineyards have been replanted to better grapes; orchards have been torn out; unlikely hillsides have been planted. Today Napa County is full of grapevines of the best Vinifera varieties.

Napa Valley is narrow, about four miles across on the average, and not especially long, stretching around thirty-five miles from the Carneros district, south of the town of Napa and across the bay from San Francisco, to Mount St. Helena, above Calistoga. On the west it is bounded by the Mayacamas Mountains and the Sonoma County line, on the east by a broken series of hills and lakes. Traditionally, the Davis scale divides Napa into three regions. The southernmost section—from the base of the valley in the Carneros district, through the town of Napa and up as far as Yountville—is held to be Region I, cool, foggy, and especially well respected for Chardonnay and Pinot Noir. The middle section, from Yountville up to Zinfandel Lane, which runs in an easterly direction from the main valley highway, Route 29, just north of Rutherford, is Region II. Here Cabernet Sauvignon is king. Finally, north of Rutherford through St. Helena and up to and beyond Calistoga is registered as Region III and is especially regarded for Petite Sirah and Zinfandel.

As a rule of thumb that definition works very well, but Napa is the part of California where most work has been done on microclimates, the place where individual vineyard wines are most often produced. Napa growers have long since gone beyond the gross Davis divisions. How many growing sections are there in Napa (or any other section of the North Coast Counties, for that matter)? Already some Napa wines are entitled to use one of eight appellations—Calistoga, Carneros, Mount Veder, Oakville, Pritchard Hill, Rutherford, Spring Mountain, and Yountville. But one publication, *The Connoisseurs' Guide to California Wines*, is on record as proposing that Napa County be accorded nineteen separate viticultural appellations. In arriving at this arrangement, the editors of the *Guide* state that they discarded one proposal listing three hundred separate designations.

The detail of this proposal need not concern us very much. The fact that there is an argument means, however, that there is something to argue about. Napa Valley growers and winemakers are so sophisticated that they are able to produce wines of special character and individuality, often in small or minute lots, to such a degree that the consumer finds himself presented with an immense range of choices.

THE MAJOR NAPA WINERIES

Most of these choices are offered by the some fifty small wineries in the valley. Not all Napa wineries are boutiques or even merely small, however. Some of the most famous names are relatively large operations. Since they first marked Napa and theirs are the Napa wines one most often encounters, we turn to them first.

In the center of the valley, just north of St. Helena, stands the headquarters of Charles Krug Winery, founded in 1861 and thus able to claim to be the oldest existing winery in the Napa Valley. Charles Krug wines were famous throughout most of North America and in some countries abroad by 1890, but debt and phylloxera destroyed Krug's fortune, and the winery fell on hard times. It was closed during Prohibition, and only started on its modern path when Cesare Mondavi bought it, giving it the alternate name of C. Mondavi & Sons.

In 1943 Mondavi and his sons, Peter and Robert, bulk-wine producers in the San Joaquin Valley, sold their Acampo winery in Lodi and purchased Charles Krug. But this change did not lead them to relinquish their interest in jug wines. Today, at St. Helena and elsewhere in the state Krug has storage capacity for about nine million gallons of wine, and well over half is bottled and sold as CK Mondavi jug wines.

Many of the CK wines originate in the San Joaquin Valley, and only Krug's top-quality wines are given the Charles Krug label. Most of the Krug wines are vintage-dated, Napa Valley appellation wines. Pride of place is taken by the Cesare Mondavi Selection Cabernet Sauvignon, made mostly from grapes grown in an Oakville vineyard of great age.

Overall, Krug is known mostly for white wines. It was Krug, for example—actually Robert Mondavi—that "invented" Chenin Blanc in 1945. Before Mondavi came along, it was not produced as a varietal at all. The style of the Krug Chenin Blanc has not changed; it is still a clean, fresh, slightly sweet wine. The Chardonnays are exceptionally well made to give them a mellow, smooth finish. Other Krug whites include a sweetish Johannisberg Riesling, a sweet and a dry Sauvignon Blanc (the latter is called Blanc Fumé), an almost dry Sylvaner, and two Sémillons, Dry Sémillon and a very sweet version, Sweet Sauternes—both of which show some of the deficiencies resulting in the recent abandonment of this varietal by most of its producers.

Krug reds are made for easy drinking, except for the Selection Cabernet Sauvignon, which is made big, soft, and with ample tannin to insure good development. The Pinot Noir, which comes from Carneros, is a sound if light example of what can be done with the grape. The Zinfandels are very fruity and drinkable immediately after release.

Charles Krug spawned the newest of the large Napa producers: Robert Mondavi Winery. As a result of a family argument in 1965, Robert Mondavi left Charles Krug to establish with his son, in 1966, the wholly new winery bearing his name. The winery, designed to resemble a Spanish mission, is located at Oakville, on the west side of Route 29, and is equipped with the latest in modern technology, including a computer that monitors the performance of the wines in the fermenting containers and storage tanks.

The computer is evidence of the fact that Mondavi is in the forefront of the wave of producers who constantly experiment to find ways to improve the quality of their wine. Thus, he has worked with cooperage of every sort in an effort to find compatibilities between wine and especially congenial fermenting and aging containers. His winery now contains about sixteen thousand small oak barrels, and even his popular red and white jug wines are given a touch of oak age.

In recent years, Mondavi has bought out its financial partner, acquired the name and stock of Oakville Vineyards—which used to be the "other" Oakville winery but went out of business in 1977—and seen its vineyard holdings rise to over eleven hundred acres and its storage capacity grow to nearly two million gallons. Finally, as a result of a protracted law case, in 1976 Robert's suit against his

Map 6. Napa Valley Wineries

brother Peter regarding Charles Krug was settled in Robert's favor, though he subsequently allowed himself to be bought out, thus severing himself entirely from Charles Krug/C. Mondavi & Sons.

Robert Mondavi is known to be quality-conscious and original. Thus just as he brought out the first Chenin Blanc at Krug, in 1966 he "invented" Fumé Blanc, a dry Sauvignon Blanc. The name Fumé Blanc caught on at once, and the dry, lean style of the varietal has been the model of many successors and imitators.

These days Mondavi tries to leave the wines alone as much as possible. For example, he filters and fines his wines less than many other producers do. Unfined and unfiltered wines are less stable, and most producers choose not to run the attendant risks. Mondavi feels that his technological control is sufficiently sophisticated to allow him to run these risks, and that his wines are richer and more true to their natural character due to the abandonment of these steps.

A perfect example of the Mondavi approach is seen in what he is doing with Pinot Noir. This difficult grape, which California wine-makers often all but give up on, is a favorite of Mondavi, and he thinks the wines he makes from Carneros grapes are certain to prove him right. The grapes are separated from the stems only after prolonged contact, and the wines, after extensive oak aging, remain intense and full-bodied, as close to Burgundies as Mondavi can get them.

Mondavi Rieslings come in different styles, late harvest, low-alcohol, and regular, soft but dry. The Cabernet Sauvignons are very carefully made, French-oak-aged wines, typical of the best that Napa Valley can offer. The Zinfandels are on the light side in style—quite the opposite of, for example, the huge Ridge Zinfandels. They are made to be drunk as soon as released. Nor surprisingly, the Chenin Blancs and Chardonnays of Mondavi are fairly close in style to those of Charles Krug.

Similar in size to Mondavi is Beaulieu Vineyard of Rutherford. Beaulieu is one of the great and most ancient names of Napa, founded in 1900 by Georges de Latour, a Frenchman and something of a rarity among the many Italians of Napa and Sonoma. Until 1969 the winery was owned and managed by members of one family, who survived during Prohibition by making wine for the church and who, consequently, were prepared to take advantage of Repeal more effectively than most other wineries.

Beaulieu thus became one of the best-known names in the United States. It also produced some of the best wines—largely as a result of hiring Russian-born, French-trained winemaker André Tchelist-cheff, who arrived at Beaulieu in 1938.

Tchelistcheff remained as winemaker at Beaulieu until 1973, and it is no exaggeration to say that no other single individual has done as much as Tchelistcheff to develop the quality of California wines—and also those of Washington and Mexico, for that matter.

Tchelistcheff's greatest contributions are threefold. First, he identified Cabernet Sauvignon as California's great red-wine-grape, and led Beaulieu and others who followed its lead to concentrate on this grape. Second, he introduced the practice of aging Cabernet Sauvignon wines in small oak barrels to give them subtlety and complexity. Finally, he trained and advised an impressive number of the leading winemakers in the industry today. His work is far from over, even though he is no longer associated with Beaulieu (his son is technical director there now), and his name as consultant constantly crops up, at Simi, Hoffman Mountain Ranch, Firestone, and elsewhere.

Tchelistcheff's greatest wines are probably the Georges de Latour Private Reserve Cabernet Sauvignons he produced, a series beginning with the vintage of 1936 that are always made from grapes picked from one vineyard near the Rutherford winery. He has said that his greatest challenge has been Pinot Noir, and he was one of the early advocates of Carneros plantings for this varietal. Beaulieu planted in Carneros early, beginning in 1963, as a result.

In 1969 a thunderclap was heard over Napa Valley. The owners of Beaulieu had sold out to Heublein, the Connecticut conglomerate that owned United Vintners and all its labels. People held their breath. How would the venerable institution survive? The answer seems to be: very well. Beaulieu and United Vinters report to different divisions of Heublein. And under the leadership of its president, Legh Knowles, Beaulieu goes very much its own, old way.

Beaulieu's way involves the production of a large variety of wines for a winery that has storage capacity of only about 1.3 million gallons and sells some two hundred fifty thousand cases of wine a year. In addition to sacramental wines, it makes sparkling wines, Sherries, and table wines. The table wines include a relatively uncommon Muscat de Frontignan, a sweet, flavorful wine, among its list of varietally labeled and vintage-dated as well as generic wines.

With respect to the latter, Beaulieu is refreshingly strict about listing the precise contents of wines not 100 percent composed of the named varietal.

The Georges de Latour Private Reserve Cabernet Sauvignon is a huge, intense, and expensive wine produced in small quantities from the one vineyard retained by the owners of Beaulieu when they sold to Heublein. An admirable wine, one of the best bargains in the field, is the regular bottling of Cabernet Sauvignon. In addition, Beaulieu makes a Cabernet Sauvignon with a 20 percent Merlot blend called Beau Tour Cabernet Sauvignon. It's very fruity and quite adequate for everyday drinking.

As one would expect from the winery that André Tchelistcheff branded, the Pinot Noirs are exceptional. Their style is fatter and more fruity than Mondavi's. The quality of Carneros Pinot Noir is especially detectable in the differences between the regular bottling, Beaumont Pinot Noir—which is 100 percent Pinot Noir from Carneros, aged for twelve months in small oak casks—and the lighter Beau Velours Pinot Noir, made from non-Carneros Pinot Noir and aged only in large casks. The Beau Velours is closer to a light Beaujolais than to a French Burgundy.

For whites, Beaulieu's Chardonnay—called Beaufort Pinot Chardonnay—is mellow, oaky, buttery. Johannisberg Riesling is made in two styles, dry and soft and, when possible, sweetly botrytised. Its Sauvignon Blanc, Chateau Beaulieu, is one of the sweetest made.

Across Route 29 from Beaulieu is Inglenook Vineyards. Between this winery and Beaulieu a considerable rivalry has existed that has been muted only recently by the common ownership of Heublein.

Inglenook dates from 1879, when a Finnish sea captain and fur trader, Gustave Niebaum, bought a vineyard, replanted it to prime varietals, and started work on a large winery. Niebaum cared little for expense; he wanted simply to produce wines that were the equal of and perhaps superior to the best produced anywhere in the world: an ambition he was satisfied to have reached before his death in 1908. The winery closed during Prohibition, but it reopened in 1933 and continued to be run on what can only be described as noble but ill-fated lines. Quality standards were so high that it was virtually impossible for the winery to break even, let alone make money.

Inglenook, one of the first wineries to use varietal labels, was the proudest of all Napa wineries and the most quality-conscious. Thus the wine world was shocked when the whole winery and almost all its vineyards were sold to United Vintners in 1964 and horrified when United Vintners was sold to Heublein in 1968. The fact that Beaulieu was sold to Heublein directly while Heublein acquired Inglenook as part of United Vintners explains how the two wineries can still function as rivals.

At first, it seemed as if the worst fears of the doubtful were justified. Two new lines of Inglenook wines were introduced: Navalle Inglenook wines, which had virtually nothing to do with Napa and were for the most part made at Asti at the Italian Swiss Colony winery, and North Coast Counties wines. Then the volume of the top-of-the-line, estate-bottled, Napa Valley wines increased dramatically, suggesting that the quality of the grapes used might not be what it once was.

Inglenook, in fact, is an example of the meaninglessness of the term "estate-bottled." Once Inglenook became part of United Vintners, the door was opened for use by Inglenook of all the Allied Growers' Napa grapes—some fifteen hundred acres of them. Calling the wines made from all these grapes estate-bottled says nothing about them.

In any case, the rot seems to have stopped. No doubt the appointment of a new young winemaker, Thomas Ferrell, in 1972 had much to do with the stabilization. Inglenook is no longer a premium house, but it has found a new role as the producer of a reliable line of wines in substantial quantity.

Inglenook's most famous wines have always been Cask bottlings of Cabernet Sauvignon and Pinot Noir. The newly made Cask wines, especially the Cabernet Sauvignon, are produced in the style of pre-United Vintners days and should be welcomed. The other wines, both Napa Valley and North Coast Counties, are made for easy drinking, the whites softish, the reds fruity rather than intense—exactly what one would expect of a winery the size of the modern Inglenook, some three million gallons.

The only Napa Valley winery larger than Inglenook is Christian Brothers, which is properly called Mont La Salle Vineyards. Though they have been in Napa only since 1930—they had been making wine since 1882 elsewhere—Christian Brothers now run the oldest uninterrupted winemaking operation in the valley, all other existing wineries having changed hands in the intervening years.

Christian Brothers is a teaching order. The after-tax income from their winemaking operations goes to support their schools and colleges. Their Napa Valley headquarters and novitiate are at Mont La Salle, about six miles from the town of Napa, partway up Mount Veeder. In addition to the Mont La Salle winery, they own an enormous and highly automated stainless-steel fermenting facility, just south of St. Helena, and the picturesque Greystone Winery, in St. Helena, which was built in the late 1880s and opened with much fanfare as the largest winery in the world. It was so large, in fact, that not until the Brothers took over in 1950 and converted it into their facility for the production of sparkling wines and aging of table wines did it become anything but a white elephant.

The Brothers have something like fifteen hundred acres of vines in Napa and another thousand in the San Joaquin Valley, where they own the largest brandy-producing winery in the country.

Christian Brothers wines are almost always blends. In fact, until 1977 they were always nonvintage blends. Guided by cellarmaster Brother Timothy, whose name is well known to all wine fanciers, blending at Christian Brothers has become a fine art. For example, one recently released Pinot Noir began with the evaluation of ninety Pinot Noirs from four different vintages and ten different vineyards. The final blend involved use of seventeen Pinot Noirs, which together totaled 85.5 percent of the resulting wine. A Cabernet Sauvignon may represent evaluation of over 130 different wines from four vintages and an actual blend of close to forty wines.

Christian Brothers is a winery of about thirty-million-gallon capacity, and not surprisingly it produces a huge range of wines, close to fifty in all. Most are cleanly made, soft, drinkable, and unexceptional.

The most interesting wines are its famous Chateau La Salle, a light, sweet wine made from Muscat de Frontignan grapes, and the Brother Timothy Special Selection wines—Cabernet Sauvignon, Gamay Noir, Pinot Noir, and Zinfandel—which have seen plenty of wood and two years in the bottle before being released. The Zinfandel is an especially good example of a light, berrylike varietal.

The Christian Brothers have been perhaps the most committed opponents of vintage dating in California. But just as consumer pressure is causing Gallo to plan to oak-age some of its wines in the near future, it has forced the Christian Brothers to respond. Thus in 1977, the Brothers released their first vintage wines, a 1973 late harvest Johannisberg Riesling with 7.7 percent residual sugar and a 1976 Gewürztraminer, nicely spicy and fruity. With the Riesling, the Brothers, perhaps thinking that having gone as far as to vintage date they might as well go all the way, even listed the single vineyard, White Ranch, from which the grapes came.

It seems that no standard cannot be breached, but in this case the change is clearly for the better.

Two other wineries round out the Napa Valley list of sizable operations: Beringer Vineyards/Los Hermanos Vineyards and Louis M. Martini.

Beringer dates to 1876, when two brothers began to make wine. The brothers, and then their descendants, made wine every year—during Prohibition they sold to the church—until the winery, its vineyards, and its picturesque Rhine House, an elegant mansion designed to look like a river house from the Beringer brothers' native Germany, were sold to the Nestlé Company.

Today, Beringer, which is situated in north St. Helena next door to the Christian Brothers' Greystone Winery, owns and leases nearly three thousand acres of vineyards and produces two lines of wines: Beringer premium wines and Los Hermanos jugs, including varietal jugs. The winemaker is Myron Nightingale, who worked for Cresta Blanca in the early 1960s when it was still in Livermore.

Beringer is another middle-of-the-road winery, with carefully made wines, somewhat similar to Inglenook's in style. The Chardonnay, for example, is aged in oak barrels of larger size than those the true premium houses use. Thus the wines are slightly oaky, fruity, and balanced, to be drunk now.

Two of Nightingale's best wines were the Centennial Cask wines that marked Beringer's centennial in 1976. The 1973 Centennial Cabernet Sauvignon was first rate, an intense version of Beringer's everyday, desirable but not complex Cabernet Sauvignons.

The last of the major Napa wineries is by no means the least. Louis M. Martini, who founded the company of that name just south of St. Helena in 1934, served an apprenticeship at Guasti in Cucamonga and at Kingsburg in the San Joaquin Valley, as well as in Italy.

In 1940 he moved to Napa, selling his interests outside the valley, and he ran his winery until he died in 1974. His son, also called Louis, and his family now are in charge. The family connection is as important in the Martini story as it is with Cesare Mondavi and his family, perhaps even more so because Louis M. stamped his mark all over his winery.

Martini was an innovator and a man of firm viticultural bias. While he felt that Napa grapes were often the best, he did not think that Napa had a monopoly on good grapes. Martini thus purchased vineyards and grapes from many sections of the state. In particular, in Sonoma County he bought and planted vineyards in the Sonoma Valley and near Healdsburg. He did the same in Carneros, and in the high, hot Chiles Valley, to the east of Napa.

From the beginning, since they were all blends of North Coast Counties wines, Martini wines have been called Mountain wines. The official appellation is California, though often the wines come from a single vineyard. Martini pioneered in the effort to identify microclimates. The fruits of this search are often bottled as Martini Special Selection wines, often idiosyncratic and almost experimental. These are available only at the winery.

Martini wines are made so that the varietal flavor shows through. The reds usually are aged in large oak tanks, the whites in stainless steel or refrigerated redwood casks. The result, while not terribly fashionable these days, is eminently successful, especially for red wines, for which Martini is best known.

The Cabernet Sauvignons are made in precisely this way; they are flavorful, fresh wines of great character. The Pinot Noir is a Martini favorite, and it was Martini who pioneered use of Carneros-grown Pinot Noir grapes. Martini is also very well known for Zinfandels and Barberas. All are made to emphasize varietal flavor and are fresh and accommodating, though in no way small.

The Martini style works best with red wines. Particularly in comparison with other whites available, the style often leaves white wines seeming somewhat pale. This is especially true of Chardonnays. Martini is the only producer of a varietal Folle Blanche, which it makes dry and fresh, and has a very attractive, dry Chenin Blanc. Its most successful white probably is the Gewürztraminer, which is spicy and a model for other producers of the varietal.

THE SMALLER NAPA WINERIES

There are more than sixty wineries in Napa. To do full justice to them all would take far too much space, and to make matters even more complicated, new ones are constantly appearing. So on our tour up and down the valley, we will merely mention some while stopping longer at others. Some will be ignored altogether. Bear in mind what was said at the beginning of chapter 6: a particular winery not mentioned does not mean it is not a worthwhile venture.

The wineries of Napa stretch along Route 29, the Wine Road, in the center of the valley, dot the Silverado Trail, which runs parallel to Route 29 on the east side of the valley, and are scattered in small pockets on hillsides—Mt. Veeder, Spring Mountain—or in valleys outside Napa proper—Pope Valley.

North of Calistoga there is only Chateau Montelena Winery on the Silverado Trail at the base of Mt. Helena. The winery actually is a restored building that dates to the late nineteenth century, and wine has been made there for many years. In 1968 it was bought by Lee Paschich, who with his partners hired Miljenko Grgich as winemaker in 1972, to make the winery fully operational. In 1974 Grgich made the notable 1973 Chardonnay that was voted first among four French white Burgundies and five other California Chardonnays at the Spurrier tasting held in Paris in 1976. Grgich left Chateau Montelena in 1977, but the new winemaster is just as well reputed: Jerry Luper, formerly of Freemark Abbe.

Chateau Montelena makes only four wines, each of which is first rate: Cabernet Sauvignon, Zinfandel, Chardonnay, and Johannisberg Riesling. Zinfandel and Johannisberg Riesling are light and fresh in style; Cabernet Sauvignons are oak-aged, intense, and tannic; Chardonnays are butter-smooth and mouth-filling.

Chateau Montelena has a three-thousand-gallon capacity. Although it is by no means tiny, its wines are hard to find because they are so highly regarded. Thus it is well to remember that it has a second label: Silverado Cellars, whose wines are less fine, but not less carefully and distinctively made.

South of Chateau Montelena, along the Silverado Trail, is Cuvaison, which has been producing Cabernet Sauvignon, Zinfandel, and Chardonnay in recent years, having settled down after a shaky start in 1970. Its winery building dates from 1974, and it buys most of its grapes from other growers.

Between Cuvaison and Route 29 stands one of the most impressive wineries, Sterling Vineyards, which visitors reach by aerial tramway, straight up for 250 feet. The buildings look like a glaring white church set in the Greek Islands, and the tower is decorated with a set of London bells. The substance behind the facade is equally impressive. Steel fermenting tanks and a huge display of oak cooperage signify the investment the operation represents.

The first plantings occurred in 1964; the first wines in 1969. The winery was built in 1973, and it has capacity of four hundred thousand gallons of wine. In 1977, Coca-Cola of Atlanta bought Sterling as its first major investment in California. Sterling wines, made until late 1978 by winemaster Richard Forman who still serves as a consultant, have done exceptionally well since they first appeared. Sterling is probably best known for its Merlot, which was introduced in 1972 and has won plaudits. It is probably the best California Merlot. Among its other reds, the Cabernet Sauvignon, made in a Bordeaux style in that Merlot is blended into the Cabernet Sauvignon, is well regarded. Of whites, the Sauvignon Blanc, lightly aged in oak, is very attractive, and the Chardonnay, Gewürztraminer, and dry Chenin Blanc are appealing. Finally, Sterling makes some good, straightforward red and white jugs, called Sterling Red and White.

A much smaller winery is to be found at the junction of Dunaweal Lane, on which Sterling is situated, and Route 29, a few miles south of Calistoga: Stonegate Winery. Stonegate produced its first wines in 1973, and makes chiefly estate-bottled Cabernet Sauvignon, Pinot Noir, Chardonnay, Sauvignon Blanc, and Chenin Blanc. Its Petite Sirah is one of the best made in California.

Diamond Mountain rears up across Route 29 from the entrance to Dunaweal Lane, and its vineyards are entitled to a separate appellation. One winery, Diamond Creek Vineyards, produces Cabernet Sauvignon from three separately named vineyards: Volcanic Hill, Red Rock Terrace, and Gravelly Meadow. Diamond Creek is a true Napa boutique, selling huge wines in minute quantities at high prices. The wines—all 100 percent estate-grown varietals—are what the connoisseur of California wines thinks the ultimate in winemaking is all about. Of course, the wines are generally unavailable!

Following Route 29 south, one passes the entrance, on the west, to Schramsberg and, on the east, to Hanns Kornell, both makers of sparkling wines, which are discussed in chapter 13.

Looming over Schramsberg is one of the most famous names in Napa, Stony Hill Vineyard, which, not coincidentally, happens to be one of the smallest wineries, with a capacity of about seven thousand gallons. Fred and Eleanor McCrea bought their vineyard property as a second home in 1943. They planted vines and in 1953 built a winery. Within a few years, their Johannisberg Rieslings, Chardonnays, and Gewürztraminers were winning awards in numbers completely out of proportion to the winery's size. One Spring Mountain Chardonnay was featured at the Paris tasting.

The McCreas—Fred died in 1977—never compromised in terms of quality or size, and they have been an example to dozens of people who have decided they could do what the McCreas did just because they did it.

Stony Hill wines are all oak-aged, but to achieve delicacy and flavor, not weight. Fred McCrea opposed adamantly the loading of Chardonnays with oak, and his wines live longer than most without the overload. The wines are available almost exclusively by mail order. Other Napa wineries eagerly buy the grapes the McCreas cannot use themselves.

To the north and west of St. Helena rises Spring Mountain, another section of Napa with its own appellation. Wineries on the mountainside include Yverdon Vineyards, Chateau Chevalier Winery, and Spring Mountain Vineyards. Closest to St. Helena is Spring Mountain, founded in 1968 but recently rehoused in a nineteenth-century mansion, Miravelle, the home of one of the more famous grapegrowers in Napa during its early days.

Spring Mountain wines were originally made in somewhat makeshift conditions, composed of other growers' grapes. However, they have been consistently well made. Now that Spring Mountain's owner, Michael Robbins, has his own vineyards coming in and a functioning, permanent winery, one can expect the Cabernet Sauvignons, Chardonnays, and Sauvignons Blancs that Robbins and his winemaker, Charles Ortman, produce to become even more steady and reliable. All the wines are oak-aged.

Beyond Spring Mountain is another handsome nineteenth-century building, reopened in 1973 as Chateau Chevalier, which produces Cabernet Sauvignon and Johannisberg Riesling. Under its second label, Mountainside Vineyards, Chateau Chevalier has produced wines since 1972. Their first wines appeared in 1976, estate-bottled Cabernet Sauvignon and Chardonnay.

Farther up the mountain still is Yverdon, which was founded in 1970 and was built stone by stone, literally, by a father and his son, Fred and Russell Aves. They also planted their own vines and even assembled their own barrels—a quite wonderful achievement by any standard—and more so considering that Fred Aves retired to Napa from a career as a manufacturer of auto parts. The wines are trustworthy, if not outstanding. At least, one can be sure one is drinking honest wines.

St. Helena proper, as we have seen, is home to Charles Krug, Beringer/Los Hermanos, and Christian Brothers' Greystone. It is also home, a little farther north than Krug, to Freemark Abbey. Freemark Abbey is no abbey and never was: the name comes from a combination of the names of the partners involved in the venture, which dates to 1968.

Freemark Abbey, which has a capacity of about fifty thousand gallons, was one of the first of the new, influential wineries in the Napa Valley. It owes its winemaking style to Hanzell, who "discovered" small French oak in Sonoma. When James Zellerbach first introduced the French idea to the United States in the middle 1950s, one of the seven partners in the venture, Bradford Webb, was consultant to Zellerbach.

From its inception, Freemark Abbey has taken second place to none—stainless-steel cold fermenters, the very latest in bottling processes, aging in small oak barrels and in small lots. All this was, to a degree, pioneering in Napa and is to be found in many other wineries today.

The results of the effort are very impressive. Freemark Abbey wines are consistent prizewinners. It was the only winery at the Paris tasting to be represented by Chardonnay *and* Cabernet Sauvignon. The Petite Sirah is especially intense, as are both regular Cabernet

Sauvignon and Cabernet Sauvignon Bosche. The latter is a single-vineyard Cabernet Sauvignon of remarkable fruit and intensity that is matched in an unusual combination of lightness of body. The winery, which used to make Pinot Noir each year, is abandoning that varietal, which will now appear solely as a Rutherford Hill (*see* below) wine.

The Freemark Abbey whites are its most famous wines. Chardonnays are aged in oak, of course, but not excessively. The idea is to bring out flavor, not to overwhelm the wine. But Freemark is best known for its Johannisberg Rieslings, and particularly for its late harvest wines. The Edelwein it produced in 1973 opened the floodgates for the production of this style of wine, as is explained in chapter 14.

South of St. Helena is Louis Martini and, close by, Sutter Home Winery and Heitz Wine Cellars' original home. Sutter Home is a family business that until 1969 sold most of its wines, at a comparatively low cost, at the winery. In 1969, however, Sutter Home unveiled Amador County Zinfandels to the world at large, especially the wines made from grapes from the Deaver Ranch. It now concentrates on Amador County Zinfandels, including a white Zinfandel, with great success, in its four-hundred-thousand-gallon-capacity winery.

Heitz Cellars is one of the most important names in Napa. Joseph Heitz first became interested in wines while serving as an airman in California during World War II. After the war he enrolled at Davis to study enology, worked at Beaulieu, and taught at Fresno. Then in 1961 he bought an old winery and a Grignolino vineyard next door to the Martini winery on Route 29.

Since then Heitz has continued to make Grignolino and even a Grignolino Rosé, but the name is associated more closely with much more important wines. Heitz made a fine beginning by purchasing and selling much of the stock of Hanzell in the early 1960s, and the winery has specialized in buying small, select lots of grapes from other growers.

In 1965 Heitz moved its main operations up into the hills behind the Silverado Trail, into a newly constructed building and a restored old winery adjacent to the new building. In 1968 he released its first Martha's Vineyard Cabernet Sauvignon. Although Heitz charged a steep price for the wine, demand for the bottling, in that vintage and thereafter, has never slackened. Probably it is the single most famous Cabernet Sauvignon. It, too, was featured in Paris.

Heitz's style calls for big wines—Cabernet Sauvignon and Chardonnay. The Cabernet Sauvignons are tannic and require age in the bottle. The Chardonnays are mouth-filling, huge, worthy followers of their Hanzell predecessors. The Zinfandels are usually only cellared, the wines having been bought from others.

Barbera is made lighter, fermented slowly and quietly, so that the fruit does not become lost. The Pinot Noirs are fruity and Burgundian, in the newer, improved style of Martini, Beaulieu, and Mondavi.

The Heitz lesser whites, Gewürztraminer and Johannisberg Rieslings, are very well made, spicy and fruity, respectively. Heitz Chablis, which always contains a measure of Chardonnay, is perhaps the winery's most popular wine. It carries all the marks of a Heitz yet is affordable!

Heitz Cellars is situated on Taplin Road, which runs into the Silverado Trail. Just before you get to the junction, a northward-running lane leads up to Joseph Phelps Vineyards. Owned by a Denver contractor, Phelps Vineyards was planted in 1973, and the handsome, wooden winery buildings were constructed a year later. Phelps has a capacity of about two hundred fifty thousand gallons, and under the direction of its German-trained winemaster, Walter Schug, is as dedicated to quality as is the smaller Freemark Abbey.

Phelps released its first wine, a fresh, light German-style 1973 Johannisberg Riesling, in 1975, thereby serving immediate notice that this was a winery requiring attention. Phelps has continued to produce excellent Rieslings, including a series of late harvest wines that are as good as any produced in California (*see* chapter 14).

Other whites produced by Phelps include an excellent Sauvignon Blanc, the obligatory Chardonnay, Pinot Noir Blanc, and Gewürz-traminer. The latter varietal is one of Phelps's best wines, both in the spicy regular bottling and in a late harvest version.

The reds include Cabernet Sauvignon, Pinot Noir—in the future of which it believes strongly—Zinfandel, and the only Syrah in the Napa. Syrah is the chief grape of the Rhône Valley, after which Petite Sirah is named, though they are only slightly, if at all, connected. Phelps's best wines, produced in very small lots, are distinguished by the Insignia label. Its very satisfactory second label is Le Fleuron.

Also in this area is Rutherford Hill Winery, the latest step in a tangled story. The story begins in the nineteenth century, with the planting of vineyards to the north of the Rutherford Hill location on a site on Howell Mountain. In 1943 the derelict vineyard was bought by J. Leland Stewart, who renamed it Souverain and made wines there until he retired in 1970. The purchasers of his operation sold it to Pillsbury, the Minneapolis milling concern. Pillsbury had great plans. It sold the old Souverain holdings to a couple, who renamed it Burgess Cellars (*see* below), and moved the winery down to the Rutherford site, calling the new winery Souverain of Rutherford. This was to be run in conjunction with the Souverain of Alexander Valley we encountered in Sonoma County.

When Pillsbury sold Souverain of Alexander Valley, it sold its Napa Valley winery, too. The new owners, who renamed it Rutherford Hill, are the partners who own Freemark Abbey. The two operations are quite separate, though it is, in a way, fair to call Rutherford Hill Freemark Abbey's second label.

Rutherford Hill has a capacity of about six hundred thousand gallons and is producing Gewürztraminer, Johannisberg Riesling, Pinot Noir Blanc, Pinot Noir, Cabernet Sauvignon, and Zinfandel. The Cabernet Sauvignon includes a proportion of Merlot, making it softer and more accessible than the big Freemark Abbey wines. At their prices, Rutherford Hill wines should be good values.

The third winery spawned in one way or another by the saga of Souverain, Burgess Cellars, is also thriving. Situated to the north-east of St. Helena, in the hills beyond the Silverado Trail, the original vineyards and winery revived by Leland Stewart are owned and operated by former pilot Tom Burgess and his wife, Linda.

Production at Burgess is small, no more than fifteen thousand cases a year, and quality is very high. Techniques differ from other premium wineries to some degree, however. For example, whites are fermented not in stainless steel, the fashionable way, but in one-thousand-gallon oak casks. After fermentation they are placed in small oak barrels, French or American. Most of the grapes are bought from other growers, whose vineyards are identified in many cases on the labels. They come from mountain vineyards, which Burgess thinks produce better and more strongly flavored grapes.

If on judges by the results, he may well be right. The dry Chenin Blanc is first rate, fruity and well finished in oak. The Chardonnays are probably Burgess Cellars' best wines, very big, aged in small oak to complement the ripeness of the grapes used. The just-sweet Johannisberg Rieslings are clean and refreshing. Even the modest Green Hungarian is a treat.

Among the reds, the Zinfandels are outstanding. They are made in a style light enough to encourage early drinking yet with sufficient tannin to allow aging, too. Cabernet Sauvignon is made in two styles, 100 percent Cabernet Sauvignon (labeled Vintage Select) and with an addition of Merlot. The former requires considerable bottle age before reaching a peak. The last red is Petite Sirah, also ready soon and effectively peppery on the palate. Unusually for the wine, the Grenache Rosé is finished dry and most appealingly.

Beyond Burgess is Pope Valley and the Pope Valley Winery. Pope Valley actually lies outside Napa Valley proper and is one of the warmest sections of Napa County. The winery, which has a thirty-five-thousand-gallon capacity, dates from 1909 but was refounded in 1972. It produces red wines chiefly, buying most of its grapes from valley growers and aging them in small cooperage. The Rosé of Zinfandel is one of its best wines.

As one travels back from Pope Valley, south along Silverado Trail, one comes to Route 128, just south of Rutherford Hill. Near the junction, actually on Conn Creek Road, is Caymus Vineyards. The owner of this winery is one of the best-known grapegrowers in Napa, Charles Wagner. Caymus has only a seventy-thousand-gallon capacity, but its reputation exceeds its size. Cabernet Sauvignons, Zinfandels, and Pinot Noirs—including a Pinot Noir Blanc—are much in demand, as are the very expensive Chardonnays. The second label of Caymus, Liberty School, is something to watch for. Wines issued under this label are first-rate values.

Beyond Caymus, farther out on Route 128, one comes to Chappellet Winery and then Nichelini Vineyards, two utterly dissimilar wineries. Chappellet was founded in 1969 by Donn Chappellet. Chappellet winery was designed by Richard Keith, the architect for several major new wineries, and it features the same sort of design as Sonoma Vineyards, a triangular pyramid, with a core of offices and work areas and "wings" housing crushing, fermenting, and storage facilities. Sheathed in Corten steel, which acquires a natural patina of rust, the building sits on Pritchard Hill, a section of Napa with its own appellation, overlooking Lake Hennessey. The building, to complete the pastoral idyl, nestles in its vineyard estate of one hundred acres.

Chappellet wines were made to begin with by Philip Togni, now at Cuvaison, and have been well received. Togni left in 1974, and his replacement also has left; but there is no sign of any lessening of quality. Pritchard Hill temperatures are cool, and Johannisberg Riesling is consequently much favored, but so are Cabernet Sauvignon, consistently well made, tannic and slow maturing; Merlot, made to be drunk after a period of aging; Chardonnay, in lesser quantities; and a good, dry Chenin Blanc.

Chappellet's second label, Pritchard Hill, is used for a very acceptable table wine called Pritchard Hill White.

Nichelini is one of the last country-style wineries left in Napa. The third-generation owner, James Nichelini, still sells most of his wine there, as have winery owners since it was built in 1890. The wines are simple and drinkable—everyday wines in the best sense of that term.

The Nichelini vineyards are beyond the winery, in Chiles Valley, a hot section of Napa County that today is attracting the attention of wineries finding the valley itself just about planted or built over. Martini, always a pioneer in microclimatic planting, has led the move, on the ground that Chiles is not warmer than Pope Valley, to the north. More Chiles Valley grapes undoubtedly will be appearing in Napa Valley wines in the future.

Just west of the Silverado Trail and due east of Oakville is one of the newest in-production Napa Valley wineries, Villa Mount Eden Winery. The vineyard dates to the nineteenth century, and the winery, which was founded in 1974, makes only estate-bottled wines. The 1974 Cabernet Sauvignon, the first red released, is an indication of the winery's intent to make substantial wines, signaled by the first two wines released, 1975 Chenin Blanc and Gewürztraminer.

The last three wineries of note on the Silverado Trail, close to Oakville, are the confusingly named Stag's Leap Wine Cellars and Stags' Leap Winery (both beneath a rock ledge named Stag's Leap (as one would expect), and Clos du Val Wine Company.

The two Stag's Leap wineries are as concerned with the confusion their similar names cause as are their consumers; as a result, the two are often in the courts. Nothing, however, has been settled as of the time of writing. In fact, the confusion is compounded by the listing by Stag's Leap Wine Cellars of Stag's Leap Vineyard as the source for some of its grapes.

The more famous of the two is Stag's Leap Wine Cellars, a one-hundred-thousand-gallon winery built in 1973 by Warren and Barbara Winiarski. It was the Stag's Leap Wine Cellars 1973 Cabernet Sauvignon that scored highest of all red U.S. wines at the 1976 Paris tasting, a tribute to Winiarski and his consultant, André Tchelistcheff. Winiarski started with Leland Stewart at Souverain and planted his first vines in 1970 on forty-one acres. The vines are not irrigated, and wines are made as naturally as possible, with a minimum of fining and filtering. All wines are finished in small oak cooperage, the Cabernet Sauvignons for about eighteen months.

Stag's Leap Wine Cellars' Johannisberg Rieslings are made, to all intents, dry. Gamay Beaujolais is a blend of that varietal and some

Pinot Noir and Napa Gamay. A small amount of Merlot, less than 10 percent in any one year, is added to the Cabernet Sauvignon. A rather tannic Merlot also is made. Needless to say, the wines are very expensive, and the second label, Hawk Crest, offers good value for money.

Stags' Leap Winery's label is Stag's Leap Vineyard. It is a smaller and less well-established operation. The first wines were made elsewhere in Napa, while it completed the winery: part of an old hotel. Both its dry Chenin Blanc and Petite Sirah are worth noting.

The last of the Silverado Trail wineries, Clos du Val, is one of the most interesting because it is modeled on a Médoc estate, producing, since 1975, two estate-bottled wines, Cabernet Sauvignon and Zinfandel. The French emphasis is convincing. The owner lives in France. The winemaker, Bernard Portet, is the son of the winemaker of Château Lafite.

Zinfandel is not made in France since the grape grows only in the United States, so there is no model for Portet to work with. The wines are very dark and tannic, deserving considerable bottle age. The Cabernet Sauvignons are made with a small admixture of Merlot, in the Bordeaux style; they are likely to be long-lived because for all their seeming softness they have a basic, tannic steeliness that makes them exceptional and, for California, unusual wines. Their quality was recognized at the Paris tasting.

To the southwest of Napa is the Carneros growing section, which is home to one winery. The appropriately named Carneros Creek Winery dates to 1972 and produced its first wine in 1975. It is fitting that the first was a well-made Pinot Noir, from Carneros vineyards. Only two other wines are made at Carneros Creek: Chardonnay, also from local vineyards, and Zinfandel, from grapes grown in the Shenandoah Valley of Amador County. The Carneros Creek Amador Zinfandels, which are vineyard-designated, are some of the best of the rich, ripe-berry-flavored wines typical of the region of origin.

To the west of the Napa Valley is the Mayacamas mountain range and the Sonoma County line. Just east of Yountville squats Mount Veeder, an extinct volcano. The best-known winery on the mountain is Mayacamas Vineyards, the highest in Napa Valley, which was founded in an amateur way in 1941. In 1968 a San Francisco banker, Robert Travers, and his partners bought the old property and began to make big wines of significant reputation in small quantities.

Mayacamas's capacity is sixty thousand gallons, and it never makes enough Cabernet Sauvignon, Chardonnay, and Chenin Blanc to satisfy the demand. The Cabernet Sauvignon appeared at the Paris tasting and, although expensive, is one of the cheapest of the very best Cabernet Sauvignons on the market.

The three wines are all estate-grown in light-bearing vineyards. In addition, Mayacamas purchases Zinfandel grapes to make a fairly light wine or one in the late harvest style, again using Amador County grapes.

Also on Mt. Veeder is Mt. Veeder Winery and Vineyards, with a capacity of fifteen thousand gallons. The first wine, from the 1972 vintage, was released in 1976.

Mount Veeder Vineyards grows only one grape, Cabernet Sauvignon, but it, too, makes Zinfandels with grapes from Amador, wines often lighter in style than those produced by other grapes from this area, an expensive Chardonnay, and a dry Chenin Blanc.

The last Mt. Veeder winery has not yet really set up shop. Veedercrest has vineyards on Mt. Veeder, and it plans to establish a winery there in time. However, since it first appeared, in the basement of its principal owner in 1972 and then after its move to Emeryville, Veedercrest has made Napa wines. Its Chardonnay was featured in the Paris tasting.

Having left Route 29 at Zinfandel Lane to travel east, we can now close the circle and continue the tour southward along the Wine Road. The first stop, still at Zinfandel Lane, is at Raymond Vineyard. Roy Raymond was with Beringer, and Martha Jane Raymond is a granddaughter of Jacob Beringer, one of the two founding Beringer brothers. They have ninety acres of vineyards planted to Cabernet Sauvignon, Zinfandel, Pinot Noir, Napa Gamay, Merlot, Chardonnay, Johannisberg Riesling, and Chenin Blanc, and they expect to reach the size of Freemark Abbey. Their wines are only just beginning to appear, but the first botrytised Johannisberg Riesling, 1975 vintage, won a gold medal at the Los Angeles County Fair. They offer especially good values in their Cabernet Sauvignons, Zinfandels, and Napa Gamays, which are well made and pleasingly priced.

Between Zinfandel Lane and Beaulieu in Rutherford one comes upon Franciscan Vineyards, another "problem winery" until recently. Franciscan, which opened in 1971, failed under two sets of owners before the substantial operation—near eight hundred thousand gallons in capacity—seems to have found its feet under its present owners, who took it over in 1975.

Franciscan Burgundy is one of the best generics around, fruity and very drinkable; it is a consistent medal winner. In terms of price, all Franciscan wines are exceptional. Partly this is due to the skill of winemaker Justin Meyer, one of the two owners; partly, to the fact that with some one thousand acres in Napa, Sonoma, and Lake Counties, Franciscan can select widely to produce a good wine. Meyer worked at Christian Brothers for a while, and his blending experience has proved invaluable.

Franciscan produces a full range of wines. Its lightly oaked Chardonnay is exceptionally pleasant, with no pretensions to hugeness. Johannisberg Riesling is made dry and barely sweet. Chenin Blanc is made with a tinge of residual sugar, and the Chablis, the grapes for which come from Rancho California, is quite dry, a fitting counterpart to the Burgundy.

Franciscan produces four Cabernet Sauvignons. Two are Napa Valley wines; both with about 20 percent Merlot; one is a Private Reserve, which is aged longer before release. The other two wines are 100 percent Cabernet Sauvignons from the Alexander Valley, one of which is also Private Reserve wine. In addition, Franciscan makes a Lodi Zinfandel and four Pinot Noirs,—two red Pinot Noirs, one Pinot Noir Blanc, and one Pinot Noir Rosé, even though Pinot Noir is a grape not viewed with much favor by Meyer.

Three wines are special to Franciscan. A Lake County Gamay Rosé; a 100 percent Carnelian Nouveau, Carnelian being a new

University of California cross of Cabernet Sauvignon, Carignane, and Grenache; and Sundance, a sweet proprietary wine made from Muscat grapes with 3.5 percent residual sugar.

South of Rutherford, Meyer and the other owner of Franciscan Vineyards own a separate twenty-thousand-gallon winery called Silver Oak Cellar. There they make only special Cabernet Sauvignons that have aged five years. The first release, in 1974, was first rate and, like the Franciscan wines, priced most reasonably.

Between Beaulieu and Franciscan is the home of a new winery, Grgich Hills Cellar, where the former Chateau Montelena wine-maker has established himself. If the late harvest 1977 Johannisberg Riesling is any guide, Grgich has not lost his touch.

Southward on Route 29 one passes Mondavi, then Domaine Chandon at Yountville, the newest sparkling wine producer (which is covered in chapter 13), before coming to Trefethen Vineyards, northwest of Napa.

Trefethen, with five hundred acres, was at first a grower only. With its cool Chardonnay vineyards it became a major supplier of grapes to Domaine Chandon. Increasingly, it is producing its own wines. The 1973 Chardonnay made under its own label was delicate and elegant, not like the commonly encountered, big, oaky Chardonnays of Napa. Trefethen also produces an elegant Johannisberg Riesling.

About a tenth of all the wineries in the United States are situated in the Napa Valley. Thus it is fitting to end this survey of California in the valley, which has held a preeminent place in wine enthusiasts' minds for so long.

10

WINERIES OF THE PACIFIC NORTHWEST
Small and Smaller

California is not the only western state that produces wine. There is even a winery in Hawaii, Tedeschi Vineyard, which was bonded in 1977. There are wineries in New Mexico and Colorado, where Franciscan of Napa Valley makes wine because one of the two partners lives in Denver. In Idaho, Ste. Chapelle Winery is producing interesting varietal wines. But the climate of most of the rest of the West does not suit large-scale production of quality winegrapes.

The exception is the Pacific Northwest—Washington and Oregon.

WASHINGTON

Grapes have been grown in Washington since the 1870s, though no concerted effort to grow them commercially was made at first because the western sections of the state were found to be, in the main, not sufficiently hospitable. However, in 1906 irrigation systems began to divert water from the Cascade Mountains eastward, and the hitherto almost desertlike Yakima Valley was found to be ideal for grapegrowing.

Significant plantings of grapes occurred—chiefly Concords and other Labrusca varietals, including one developed in Washington itself, Belle Isle. Washington now has more than twenty thousand acres planted to grapes, most of which are used for grape products other than wines or shipped, in concentrate form or in refrigerated containers, direct to the big producers of such wines as Cold Duck in California's San Joaquin Valley. Both United Vintners and Gallo purchase huge quantities of Concords from Washington.

Today Washington is the third largest producer of grapes in the country, after California and New York, though it has half New York's vineyard acreage. In 1977, Washington's Concord harvest, in fact, exceeded New York's, though this was due chiefly to problems with New York weather. If the demand were there—but it is not—Washington could plant tens of thousands of additional acres to Labruscas with no difficulty.

There is a growing demand for fine table wines from Washington State, which is a new and most interesting development.

Although not much was done until recently, it has been known for years that the Yakima Valley and Columbia River basin could produce fine *Vitis vinifera* grapes. Researchers at the Prosser Station of the University of Washington and grapegrowers have pointed to the fact that the Yakima Valley is roughly the same latitude as northern Bordeaux and southern Burgundy. To such people the only problem was the winters. In one winter out of six the temperature falls below -12 degrees F. Otherwise, Washington, they said, enjoyed advantages California did not: in particular, longer and yet cooler summer days during the growing season with less intense heat. These advantages were enough to ensure that, along with the hardy Labruscas, a few acres of Vinifera grapes were always to be found from which a few wineries and private individuals made table wine. They coped with winters usually by burying the vines in the ground so that they froze solid in the winter and thus survived.

All this changed when Leon D. Adams, the historian of the wine industry and founder of the Wine Institute in California, encountered some excellent homemade Grenache Rosé in Seattle. In conversation with Victor Allison, the manager of the American Wine Growers winery, Adams suggested that good wines could be made in Washington if the Washington industry would only get some expert advice.

Adams suggested that André Tchelistcheff be of great help. Taking Adams at his word, Allison persuaded Tchelistcheff to visit Washington in 1967. Tchelistcheff liked none of the commercially made wines, but he tasted another homemade wine, a Gewürztraminer, and said it was the best U.S. Gewürztraminer he had ever encountered. He thereupon took on the job of getting the Washington industry on the right footing.

Meantime, technologists discovered that the winter problem could be solved by cutting off the water supply to the grapes in the late summer, allowing the older vines to become dormant before the cold struck. Now only young vines are covered. The hardiness of the vines is no doubt improved by the fact that Washington vines are planted on their own roots, the soil being phylloxera-free.

The combination of Tchelistcheff's advice and the solving of the winter problem resulted in a remarkable flowering of an exciting new industry.

The leader in Washington is American Wine Growers, and its story is indicative of the Washington story. In 1974 the company, renamed for its wine label, Ste. Michelle Vintners, was bought by the enormous U.S. Tobacco Company, which promptly committed millions of dollars to the purchase of new vineyards and the construction of a two-million-gallon winery. It is elegantly designed to resemble a château (again!), and located over a hundred miles from the vineyards, at Woodinville, about fifteen miles northwest of Seattle.

Map 7.   Wine Centers in the Pacific Northwest

The winery alone cost more than six million dollars, and in addition, Chateau Ste. Michelle—its newest name—now owns eight hundred acres planted to Cabernet Sauvignon, Pinot Noir, Chardonnay, Johannisberg Riesling, Chenin Blanc, Gewürztraminer, Muscat, Sauvignon Blanc, Merlot, and Grenache. Its emphasis is on the production of white wines.

The Ste. Michelle wines, the only Washington State wines distributed in a significant way in the United States, began to appear in 1967 and have rapidly become accepted as being as good as those of any California winery of comparable size.

Ste. Michelle has been most successful with Johannisberg Rieslings, Sauvignon Blancs, and Gewürztraminers, particularly the latter, which bears out Tchelistcheff's enthusiasm for the state as a source of the varietal. Botrytis is no stranger to Washington, and Ste. Michelle produced a 1977 Riesling with 8.4 percent residual sugar.

Other Ste. Michelle whites include Chenin Blanc, Chardonnay—which was produced first in 1975 made in a very light, clean style—Sémillon Blanc, aromatic and full, and Chablis, made with a good dose of Sémillon.

The Cabernet Sauvignon is lighter and more fruit-filled than most California wines, though backed with plenty of tannin. The winery's Pinot Noir is used in its sparkling wines to produce a Blanc de Noir sparkling wine in the traditional manner (*see* chapter 13). Some years Chardonnay is used in the sparkling wine; other years it is absent from the cuvée. Finally, Ste. Michelle makes a good dry Grenache Rosé.

There are about ten other wineries in Washington State, though none is anywhere as large as Ste. Michelle. For a while Seneca Foods, a large New York State food concern, operated one of its three Boordy Vineyards in Prosser—the other two were in Maryland and New York—but it closed the winery in 1976. Thus after Ste. Michelle one drops to the level, in size and philosophy, of the boutique.

The best known is Associated Vintners, which is a partnership of enthusiasts, the leading lights among whom are the makers of the Grenache Rosé that interested Adams and of the Gewürztraminer that excited Tchelistcheff. Associated now has a thirty-thousand-gallon winery at Redmond, outside Seattle. The group has been growing grapes and making wine since 1961, and its label has a wide specialist following, especially for Gewürztraminer and Johannisberg Riesling.

The lesser-known wineries include the following:

Hinzerling Vineyards in Prosser has a vineyard that dates to 1971 and a winery to 1976. Hinzerling is especially well known for its Gewürztraminer, made in three styles: dry, late harvest—the 1977 had 6 percent residual sugar—and Der Sonne ("the sun" in German), a selected-cluster, late harvest wine. The latter wine, which in 1977 had 10 percent residual sugar, was made in a novel way. Partially botrytised clusters of grapes were left in trays in the sun. Honeybees, feeding on the juice, carried botrytis spores from affected grapes to those not affected. Thus Hinzerling produced an induced Botrytis Riesling through entirely natural means! The Chardonnay, lightly aged in oak, is a huge—15 percent alcohol—

wine. It is now developing some interesting Cabernet Sauvignon.

Preston Wine Cellars, Pasco, dates to 1976. It is already making some rich, full Chardonnays and also has made first-rate Fumé Blancs and Gewürztraminers. The reds have not yet been released.

Bingen Wine Cellars, Bingen, dates to 1974; Leonetti Wine Cellar, Walla Walla, to 1977; Manfred J. Vierthaler Winery, Sumner, to 1976.

There are a few fruit and berry wine producers in Washington and one that produces fruit and table wines, Alhambra Wine Company, which dates from 1935 and is located in Selah, near Yakima. Its table wines are all Labrusca wine of no special note.

OREGON

While Washington State has more than twenty thousand acres of vineyards and room for ten times that number, Oregon has only about one thousand acres. On the other hand, Oregon's acreage is almost all planted to Vinifera varietals, and recent developments suggest that there is even greater ferment in the state than in Washington.

Already more than twenty wineries are functioning in Oregon, and another ten or so are scheduled to open. None dominates in the way that Ste. Michelle dominates in Washington, and the way seems open for all sorts of interesting developments.

One of the most interesting is the strong stand that the state liquor control board has taken regarding appellation. At the behest of winemakers, the commission has ruled that varietal content must be at least 90 percent of the total composition. An exception is Cabernet Sauvignon, not much produced in Oregon, for which the level drops to 75 percent, provided the balance is made up with other Bordeaux varieties such as Merlot.

Generic labels are not permitted at all. An appellation must be used—American, Oregon, a county name, or Willamette Valley, Rogue Valley, or Umpqua Valley—and the grapes in the wine must have come *entirely* from that region.

It will be readily seen that these regulations are far stricter than the federal regulations that go into effect on January 1, 1983 (*see* chapter 4). They indicate that Oregon wines, by their makers' decree, will be produced to high standards and will be worthy of serious attention—assuming one can get hold of them.

Oregon's viticultural tradition goes back to the nineteenth century, but the current surge in winery establishment had very little to build on. One or two Labrusca producers remained in existence, but their constituency was and stays extremely small. Likewise, there is a strong tradition for making fruit and berry wines, an area in which the Honeywood Fruit Winery in Salem, the Henry Endres Winery in Oregon City, Mount Hood Winery in Mount Hood, and the Nehalem Bay Wine Company on the ocean play leading roles.

The Vinifera pioneer in Oregon is Richard Sommer, who took some courses in Davis in the 1950s and then in 1961 settled in the Umpqua Valley at Roseburg. He bonded his winery in 1963, and in 1975 it became the Hillcrest Vineyard, with a capacity of forty thousand gallons.

Sommer grows Johannisberg Riesling and Cabernet Sauvignon chiefly on his own ten acres and a further leased ten acres. In addition, he grows Chardonnay, Sauvignon Blanc, Zinfandel, Pinot Noir, Sémillon, and Gewürztraminer. Hillcrest chiefly produces Johannisberg Riesling, in both a slightly sweet and a botrytised version, but it also produces Gewürztraminer, Fumé Blanc, Chardonnay, and small quantities of Rosé of Cabernet Sauvignon, Cabernet Sauvignon, Zinfandel, Pinot Noir, and Gamey Beaujolais.

The Umpqua Valley, in the southeast part of the state, was represented solely by Richard Sommer for several years. However, his success encouraged others. In 1969 Paul and Mary Bjelland built a winery and proceeded to make both berry wines—especially blackberry—and Cabernet Sauvignon, Johannisberg Riesling, Chardonnay, and Sauvignon Blanc in a fifteen-thousand-gallon facility.

Jonicole Vineyards, a tiny winery, arrived on the scene in 1973, putting its first wines on the market in 1977, all 100 percent varietal Cabernet Rosés, Cabernet Sauvignons, and Chardonnays.

There are other vineyards in the Umpqua Valley now, and clearly the area has marked itself out for development, especially for white wines. However, the largest concentration of wineries in Oregon is to be found in the Willamette Valley, southwest of Portland.

The first winery to be built there, actually in the valley of a feeder river, the Tualatin, was the Charles Coury Vineyards. Coury, a Davis graduate, moved to David Hill near Forest Grove in 1966 and released his first wines in 1972. David Hill was established as a winegrowing locality by the turn of the century, and a Riesling from David Hill won a medal at the 1904 St. Louis World's Fair. To Coury it was cool enough to grow the grapes that really interested him: Johannisberg Riesling, Chardonnay, and Pinot Noir.

The winery will have an eventual capacity of two hundred thousand gallons, and Coury has nearly sixty acres of vines. He produces Johannisberg Rieslings, some botrytised, Gewürztraminers, Chardonnays, Sylvaners, Pinot Noirs, Rosés of Pinot Noir, and Gamay Beaujolais.

A second Forest Grove winery is Tualatin Vineyards. Founded in 1972, it has a capacity of fifty thousand gallons and sixty acres of developed vineyards. The winemaker, William Fuller, formerly was winemaker with Louis Martini, and his sure hand can be seen in the first releases: Johannisberg Riesling, Gewürztraminer, Chardonnay, Pinot Noir, Rosé of Pinot Noir, and Petite Sirah. His dry Muscat of Alexandria is impressive.

Of a similar size and close by, in Hillsboro, is Oak Knoll Winery, founded in 1970. Oak Knoll is best known for fruit wines, but has ventured into the table wine business with Zinfandel, Pinot Noir, Gewürztraminer, and Riesling. All grapes are bought from other growers.

Ponzi Vineyards of Beaverton was founded in 1970. A family affair, it has a capacity of seven thousand gallons. It produces the expected Oregon wines, plus a white Pinot Noir and a Pinot Gris, which seldom is encountered as a varietal.

Farther down the valley at Dundee is Knudsen-Erath Winery,

which is quite "old," having been founded in 1967. It has a capacity of one hundred thousand gallons and eighty acres of vineyards; plus André Tchelistcheff as a consultant.

Knudsen-Erath produces some excellent wines, one of the best being Pinot Noir. It also makes Johannisberg Riesling, Gewürztraminer, some lesser wines, including a white Pinot Noir, and the only Oregon sparkling wine, made from Chardonnay and Pinot Noir. The winery uses four labels: Erath Vineyards, Knudsen Vineyards, Knudsen-Erath, and Willamette Cellars.

A second Dundee winery is The Eyrie Vineyards, eighteen acres and twenty thousand gallons. Its first wines appeared in 1970, and it produces Pinot Noir and Chardonnay—both of which are aged exclusively in French oak barrels—Pinot Gris, Johannisberg Riesling, Sauvignon Blanc, and Gewürztraminer.

One of the newest Oregon wineries is Amity Vineyards, in the town of Amity, which was founded in 1976. This winery has a capacity of fifteen thousand gallons. It concentrates on Pinot Noir which it makes largely in a nouveau style—it was the first winery in the United States to do so—and Johannisberg Riesling, which it makes dry not sweet.

None of Oregon's wineries is large, and few ship out of state. Those that do ship to Washington State, where some Oregon wineries buy grapes (and thus lose their Oregon appellation), and California. But times are changing. Plans are afoot to enter major markets in the rest of the country.

Meantime, in Oregon developments proceed so fast it is impossible to keep up. By the end of 1979 some ten new wineries are likely to have gone into operation. One of them, Sokol Blosser Winery, of Dundee, will be making wines from vineyards planted in 1971; others will be much less well-prepared. But however much or little they are prepared, they are coming: Adelsheim Vineyard, first vintage 1978; Valley View Vineyards, the first Rogue River winery since Prohibition but not the last; Côtes des Colombe Vineyards and Elks Cove Vineyards, both in Washington County, west of Portland; Humbug Winery, a new Roseburg operation, first vintage 1978; Forgeron Vineyard ... Honey House Winery ... Century Home Wine ...

11

NEW YORK WINERIES
All Things to All People

California has more than six hundred thousand acres of vineyards. The next largest grapegrowing state, New York, has fewer than fifty thousand, something like one-fifteenth of the acreage of California. In a bad New York year, the third largest state, Washington, grows more grapes than New York State. In other words, the drop in size from California to New York is enormous.

Regardless of the drop, New York's industry is important and, as the title of this chapter suggests, varied. The variety is manifested in many ways, but chiefly in the types of wine produced. New York was and still is to a great extent a producer of Labrusca grapes, especially Concord, but it also has many acres planted to French hybrids and small but important plantings of *Vitis vinifera* grapes.

Wines are produced in New York from all three types of grapes, and from blends of them. New York's experience with French hybrids and, especially, Vinifera grapes has been of great importance to winemaking in states with somewhat similar climates, from the Northeast to the Middle West.

Vinifera grapes have always played a great part in New York's history because New York State law, recognizing the difficulty winemakers would have if forced to make wines exclusively from Labrusca grapes, allows blending of up to 25 percent of non-New York State grapes with those grown in the state. Traditionally, this balance has been made up by California, where New York wineries buy huge quantities of bulk wines each year. The difference between "then" and "now" lies in the fact that the Vinifera wines bought in California are blended into typical New York wines. The new New York Vinifera plantings are being used to produce premium varietal, estate-bottled, vintaged wine.

Finally, to add to the complexity of New York, one may note that kosher wines, or sweetened Concord wines, were invented in New York, which is still their largest producer.

Five sections of New York State are known for their grapes. Two are major—Finger Lakes and Chautauqua. Three are minor—Hudson Valley, Niagara, and Long Island.

FINGER LAKES REGION

About fifty miles south of Rochester, in west-central New York, are the Finger Lakes: long, thin lakes running north and south. It was discovered in the early nineteenth century that they have a modifying effect on winter weather, allowing grapes to be cultivated. The region is extensive, but there are six chief lakes. Starting in the east, they are Skaneateles, Owasco, Cayuga, Seneca, Keuka, and Canandaigua. Vineyards are to be found throughout the region, but most growing and winemaking occur close to lakes Seneca, Keuka, and Canandaigua.

The wineries of the Finger Lakes region make most New York State wine and have a history stretching back to 1829, when an Episcopalian priest planted Labrusca vines in his garden in Hammondsport, at the foot of Lake Keuka.

The first plantings established a pattern that was not to be altered until the 1950s. The Finger Lakes grew Labruscas, Concords, Isabellas, Dutchesses, Ives, Delawares, Niagaras, Missouri Rieslings, Noahs. The list goes on. The first commercial winery established, Pleasant Valley Wine Company—which arrived on the scene in 1860 at Hammondsport—became known for its Great Western sparkling wines, establishing an emphasis in New York on sparkling wines. (Although sparkling wines are dealt with as a category in chapter 13, one cannot deal with New York and especially the Finger Lakes without paying attention to them.)

Great Western arrived just in time to take advantage of the collapse of the Cincinnati wine industry developed by Nicholas Longworth, and its sparkling wines rapidly took the place of Longworth's famous Sparkling Catawba.

Since 1961 the Pleasant Valley Wine Company has been owned by the neighboring Taylor Wine Company but is operated as an independent arm of Taylor. The chief wines are still bottle-fermented, transfer-process sparkling wines, the best of which is dry Naturel and almost dry Brut. The sweeter Special Reserve and Extra Dry—the Extra Dry being the sweeter of the two—do not come off so well.

In addition, Great Western markets a line of Labrusca varietals—including Catawba, its first wine, Concord, Dutchess Rhine, Delaware, Niagara, Diamond, and Isabella (a rosé)—and a line of French hybrids: three reds—Chelois, Baco Noir, and the recently released De Chaunac—and one white—Aurora. Neither the heavier Baco Noir nor the lighter Chelois really is as good as other such hybrid varietals; the Aurora is sweet. The vintage De Chaunac is an appealing red wine; the Dutchess Rhine perhaps the best white.

One New York State law permits wine sugaring, a practice prohibited in California, as we have seen. Sugaring is not much respected by any winemaker or wine drinker. In consequence, one may assume that wines that can stand on their own, and not require the addition of sugar to make them palatable, are better than those made sweet through the addition of sugar.

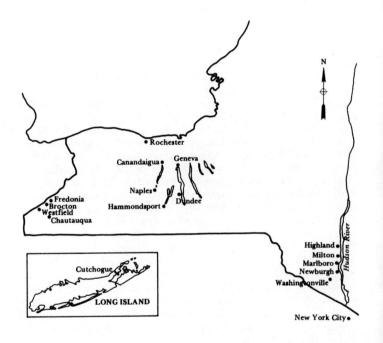

Map 8. New York's Wine Regions

When one comes to the level of the Great Western jug wines, produced under the Valley label, California jugs almost always offer better value for money, with a few exceptions.

Great Western also is a producer of fortified wines, discussed as a category in chapter 15. It uses a modified *solera* system for aging its Ports and Sherries and produces one of the better New York State lines of such wines.

The Taylor Wine Company, also in Hammondsport, was founded in 1880 by Walter Taylor, a cooper. In 1961 they bought out Pleasant Valley/Great Western, and in turn, in 1977, were bought by Coca-Cola of Atlanta.

With a capacity of thirty million gallons, Taylor is the largest eastern winery and the nation's largest producer of bottle-fermented, transfer-process sparkling wines. Until very recently all Taylor wines were Labrusca-flavored, but Taylor invested heavily in plantings of French hybrids in the 1950s and 1960s. Consequently, the Labrusca flavor has become increasingly muted for the most part.

Taylor sparkling wines are the company's most popular and best products. Brut is the best of the line, exhibiting only a trace of Labrusca foxiness and the barest hint of sweetness. The other sparkling wines—Dry, Pink, Cold Duck, Sparkling Burgundy—are less satisfactory.

Taylor produces Sherries and Ports from Labruscas; both are baked and none is very appealing, except in terms of price. It also produces undistinguished vermouths and a bottled Sangria.

Taylor does best in simple table wines. Its White, Gold, and Rosé Lake Country wines are chiefly Labruscas, and Red is largely French hybrid. All slightly sweet, these are some of the better New York State wines available.

The problems and possibilities of New York State wineries were brought to the fore by Taylor in 1978 when it introduced its California Cellars line of Rhine, Rosé, Chablis, and Burgundy. The uproar about the advertising campaign that launched the line, involving use of competitors' names and wines, was a "first" in the business. It prompted law suits and protests and tended to distract attention from the introduction of these wines.

The wines are sold by a New York State winery but are 100 percent California generics. Taylor recognizes that it is impossible to grow grapes in needed quantities in the East and that the Labrusca audience is not growing. The move also shows what can happen in big business. California Cellars are Taylor wines made by Richard Peterson of The Monterey Vineyard at the Franzia Brothers plant in the San Joaquin Valley. Franzia is owned by Coca-Cola of New York; Taylor and The Monterey Vineyard are owned by Coca-Cola of Atlanta. Judging from this massive cooperative venture, one can fairly assume that the big wineries are going to get a lot bigger.

The movement to bigness exemplified by the introduction of Taylor California Cellars wines does not, however, mean that middle- and small-sized wineries will disappear. Again New York exemplifies the truth of this statement.

The third Hammondsport winery, for example, is Bully Hill, one hundred twenty thousand gallons. Its owner, Walter S. Taylor, claims that Bully Hill is the "real" Taylor winery. A grandson of the founder, he was fired from Taylor Wine Company in 1970 for attacking its policies. Thereupon, he and his father set up their own winery and a wine museum to commemorate the founder of the Taylor Wine Company.

Walter Taylor loves a scrap. He has been feuding for years with the Taylor Wine Company over the use he may make of his own name. The legal compromise in effect now permits him to use his signature on his label provided he also list an "appropriate disclaimer" to any relationship with Taylor Wine Company on the label.

All the above is grist to Walter Taylor's publicity mill, which he uses with great skill to draw attention to his winemaking philosophy—he uses fewer chemicals than many winemakers, including Taylor, and no out-of-state wines.

Taylor's wines are chiefly French hybrids. All Bully Hill wines are vintage-dated and are either estate-bottled or "regional"—that is, New York State—wines. Regional wines appear under the Walter S. Taylor label. The newest wine is a Brut sparkling wine made from the Seyval Blanc grape. In addition to a line of well-made estate-bottled and regional jugs, Bully Hill produces French hybrid varietal wines—Baco Noir, Chancellor Noir, Chelois Noir, Seyval Blanc, and Aurora Blanc. Of these, the Chancellor Noir is one of the best.

Just outside Hammondsport is the third major winery in the area, Gold Seal Vineyards, founded as Urbana·Wine Company in 1865. Gold Seal's specialty has always been sparkling wines, and it has been directed almost from inception by European-trained winemakers.

Its most famous winemaker, and still honorary president, is Charles Fournier, who in 1934 was hired away from Veuve Clicquot, the famous Champagne house in Rheims. At Gold Seal, Fournier pioneered in many ways. His first-rate sparkling wines are discussed in chapter 13. For New York winemakers, Fournier is probably best regarded for having noted the work of Philip Wagner of Maryland, the popularizer of French hybrid vines in the United States, and, beginning in 1944, planted many commercial vineyards in the Finger Lakes area to hybrid vines.

Fournier's other significant claim to fame is that he was largely responsible for the introduction of *Vitis vinifera* grapes to New York and the East.

The real pioneer in this area is Dr. Konstantin Frank. It was Charles Fournier who first employed this "crazy Russian" who believed Vinifera vines could be grown where everyone "knew" they could not. Thus it was Gold Seal that first produced Vinifera varietals, Chardonnay and Johannisberg Rieslings, in 1959, from experimental acreage planted by Frank.

Gold Seal still makes Johannisberg Rieslings—occasionally even a late harvest botrytised version—and Chardonnays. But the commitment to Vinifera varietal wines is slight; it still feels that it is too risky to rely on Vinifera grapes in New York. It does not matter. The breakthrough occurred. Today, many wineries in New York and elsewhere, apart from Gold Seal, have acreage planted to Vinifera grapes. Great Western, for example, has small vineyards of Johannisberg Riesling and Chardonnay.

Other than sparkling wines, which range from those mentioned to Cold Duck and Spumante, Gold Seal markets a strong line of Labrusca wines, including its most popular table wine, Pink Catawba, Red and White Catawba, Concord, and two jugs called Henri Marchant Labrusca Red and White. None of the Labruscas is dry; all are marked by a considerable measure of the foxy taste of this grape family.

In recent years, Gold Seal has introduced a line of seven American generics with such names as Rhine Wine, Dry Sauterne, Vin Rosé, White Burgundy, Burgundy, Chablis Rosé, and Chablis. Gold Seal owns substantial acreage in California, in Monterey County and San Joaquin Valley, and its new jugs are the result of that investment. The best are Chablis and White Burgundy, both dry.

Finally, Gold Seal has a line of fortified wines and a Charles Fournier Chablis Nature, of which, after its top-of-the-line sparkling wines, Gold Seal and Fournier are most proud. Chablis Nature is a dry white wine made from a blend of Vinifera, French hybrid, and Labrusca grapes of the sort used in most Gold Seal sparkling wines, analogous to the still white wine that champagne makers in France and Domaine Chandon in Napa produce.

After Gold Seal, one must turn to Dr. Konstantin Frank's Vinifera Wine Cellars. Frank is a Russian-born German viticulturist whose experience in grapegrowing, before he reached the United States, was undergone in the Ukraine, where he successfully grew Vinifera grapes in an environment that, like that of New York State, can exhibit extreme cold in winter.

Frank arrived in New York City in 1951, virtually penniless and without contacts. In time he made his way to the New York State grape research station, at Geneva, in the Finger Lakes region above Lake Seneca. There he tried to persuade researchers that Vinifera grapes would grow in New York. In time his importunate pleadings came to the attention of Charles Fournier, who hired Frank in 1953 to test his theories. Frank felt above all that fine Vinifera vines would grow if he could obtain sufficiently hardy Vinifera root stock. In Quebec he found the roots and used them to begin his Gold Seal vineyards.

Frank succeeded at Gold Seal, where his vineyards of Chardonnay and Johannisberg Riesling still flourish, even through the coldest winters. However, he parted from his friend, Charles Fournier, and set out to plant his own vineyards and make his own wines.

The first Vinifera Wine Cellars wine was released in 1965 when Frank served notice that he would produce only Vinifera wines. He now grows, in addition to the accepted Chardonnay and Johannisberg Riesling, such New York Vinifera grapes as Cabernet Sauvignon, Pinot Noir, and Pinot Gris. In addition, he has experimented with plantings of several other grapes including varieties from Eastern Europe not otherwise known to growers in this country, vines with the names of Furmint (Hungary), Serksiya (Ukraine), and Rkatsiteli (Bulgaria).

Frank is evangelical about his wines and Vinifera growing, though in the Finger Lakes region only Gold Seal produces a substantial quantity of such grapes. He has produced not only Chardonnays and Johannisberg Rieslings, which many smaller wineries now are producing in the East and Midwest, but also Gewürztraminer, Pinot Noir, Cabernet Sauvignon, Gamay Beaujolais, and Muscat Ottonel, a rich dessert wine. The wines are uniformly praised for their quality and lamented for their prices— especially the late harvest Johannisberg Rieslings, at times as great as the greatest Rhine wines and priced accordingly. In 1965, Frank released a 1961 wine called Trockenbeerenauslese that cost $45. He said it was worth the price, and he was right. But winemakers and the public shook their heads.

The last Hammondsport winery, appropriately called the Hammondsport Wine Company, was recently purchased by the Canandaigua Wine Company, at the north end of the Canandaigua Lake. It will continue to be used chiefly to make sparkling wines.

Canandaigua Wine Company claims to be one of the five largest wine producers in the country. It certainly is very large, its New York operation being only one of its wineries. Dating to 1945, it was first primarily a bulk-wine producer and is best known today for two labels, Virginia Dare and Richard's.

The story of Captain Paul Garrett and his Virginia Dare wine was told in chapter 1. In the early twentieth century the Scuppernong-based wine was the most popular in the country. Garrett surfaced in the San Joaquin Valley and particularly in Cucamonga, where he kept his operation going during Prohibition with Fruit Industries and Vine-Glo, the wine concentrate sold to home winemakers. After Prohibition, the shortage of Scuppernong grapes led to the conversion of Virginia Dare wine. It became a blend of California and New York grapes, and eventually, after Garrett's 1940 death, disappeared from the market, a disused label of the Guild Wineries of Lodi.

Mack Sands, owner of Canandaigua Wine Company, recovered the name from Guild and reintroduced the label. But this time Virginia Dare was no longer a particular wine but the label of a line of New York State red, white, and pink wines—all sweet and all far removed from the original Virginia Dare.

Canandaigua owns wineries in several states. In Virginia it owns Richard's Wine Cellars and produces its famous Richard's Wild Irish Rose, a rosé that comes both in a fortified (20 percent alcohol) version and as a table wine. Both are sweet and grapey, tasting strongly of Concord.

In South Carolina, Canandaigua owns the largest winery, the Tenner Brothers Winery, which makes fruit, Labrusca, and Muscadine wines. In California, it owns the Bisceglia Brothers Wine Company of Madera, which is used mostly to produce bulk wine for the eastern branches of the company.

The other Lake Canandaigua winery is at the south end, at Naples. Widmer's Wine Cellars, founded by two Swiss brothers, dates to 1888. It now is owned by a British company. Widmer's, prompted by Frank Schoonmaker, became the first eastern winery to use varietal names and still produces many of the wines Schoonmaker singled out. Of particular note is its Niagara Labrusca, called Lake Niagara, a moderately sweet, crisp white wine; Moore's Diamond, an almost dry white; Pink Catawba, a sweet rosé; and Isabella, a rather full, sweet rosé.

Widmer's produces bulk-process sparkling wines of unexceptional character and a long list of California-style jugs, a line due to significant investment in acreage in Alexander Valley, Sonoma County.

The best wines may well be its Ports and Sherries. It has a huge *solera* on the roof of its Naples winery, and the barrels remain outside summer and winter. Widmer's wines, as a result, are probably the best fortified wines produced in the East.

Widmer's has a five-million-gallon capacity and is the last of the big Finger Lakes wineries. But there are several smaller wineries, some of which have opened as a result of the New York State Farm Winery Law that became effective in 1976. The law reduced the hitherto prohibitive state tax on wineries to a manageable $125 per year and allowed any wine produced wholly by a small winery to be sold on its premises.

The so-called farm wineries began to proliferate. More than ten opened in the first year, several in the Finger Lakes region. One of the first was the twenty-three-thousand-gallon Glenora Wine Cellars at Dundee, which produces Labrusca, French hybrid, and Vinifera wines. A second was a Vinifera winery in Hammondsport, Heron Hill Vineyards.

Other wineries are planned, but they probably will not overshadow even the smallest of established wineries—Penn Yann Wine Cellars of Penn Yan, at the top of Lake Keuga (Labrusca wines); Villa d'Ingianni Winery of Dundee, on the east shore of Lake Keuga (Labrusca, French hybrid, and Vinifera wines; varietal wines appear under the Villa label); and O-Neh-Da Vineyard of Conesus near Hemlock Lake.

O-Neh-Da is owned by the Society of the Divine Word and makes wine chiefly for church use. However, Barry Wine Company, which manages the operation, sells the excess production of Labrusca and French hybrid wines under the Barry label.

CHAUTAUQUA REGION

This section of New York on the shores of Lake Erie really forms part of a single New York-Pennsylvania-Ohio-Lake Erie region. It produces almost one-half of the grapes grown in the state, but far less wine than the Finger Lakes region because so much of the Chautauqua harvest is used for grape jellies and beverages other than wine.

Chautauqua stands and falls on the Concord grape. Plantings of Labrusca grapes began in the early eighteenth century, and several wineries flourished.

Concords, which actually were first grown in the Massachusetts town of that name, were introduced to Chautauqua more to answer the needs of the pasteurized grape industry and as an alternative for growers than to fuel the wine industry. They would not have to grow "evil" winegrapes if they were able to grow "good" Concord.

After Prohibition, wineries slowly began to recover, and grape-growers found their Concords in increased demand, especially for kosher wines and also because they were the most typical in taste of all Labrusca winegrapes.

Kosher wines were "invented" in New York. These wines, essentially simple Concord wines with sugars added, had been produced according to Jewish sacramental law for many years. But as people came back to wine after Prohibition, they discovered the sweet grapey taste of kosher wines and began to drink them as everyday wines.

One of the leading companies involved in kosher wine production is Monarch Wine Company, which makes wines under the Manischewitz label. Monarch has a five-million-gallon facility in Brooklyn. It owns the substantial Freedonia Products Company in Chautauqua which ships grape juice to Brooklyn. The company makes a line of Light Concord Red, White, and Pink wines and several sweet, Concord-based sparkling wines.

Monarch's chief competitor is the Mogen David Company of Chicago, owned by Coca-Cola of New York. Mogen David has a five-million-gallon winery in Chicago and another three-million-gallon winery in Westfield, actually in Chautauqua.

Other major kosher wineries are Schapiro's Wine Company in Manhattan and Royal Wine Corporation in Brooklyn and its subsidiary, Kedem Winer of Milton in the Hudson River Valley.

Also in Westfield is Frederick S. Johnson Vineyards, which makes estate-bottled, French hybrid wines in a one hundred-thousand-gallon winery. All wines are dry except the two rosés, Vin Rosé and Sweet Rosé. The chief wines are vintage-dated, estate-bottled Seyval Blanc, Aurora Blanc, Delaware, Chancellor Noir, and Cascade Rouge. There are also two dry jugs; Vin Rouge and Dry White. Johnson's best wine probably is the Delaware, which was made in 1975 in a late harvest style as well as the usual dry table style.

There are several new farm wineries in the area, including Woodbury Fruit Farm, which makes exceptional Vinifera wines, and Merrit Estate Winery, which concentrates on French hybrids.

NIAGARA, HUDSON VALLEY, AND LONG ISLAND

Although approximately three thousand acres are planted to Labruscas, French hybrids, and Vinifera grapes, no winery is functioning in the Niagara County at the time of writing. Probably the farm winery law will prompt the founding of a number in the near future. It most certainly has done so in the Hudson River Valley to the north of New York City.

The oldest winery in the country is the Brotherhood Corporation, founded by a charismatic religious group in 1839 in Washingtonville. The sect, rent by schism and opposition from its neighbors, moved to Brocton, in Chautauqua, and then to Sonoma County, where it produced Fountain Grove wine, a label now owned by Martini & Prati.

Brotherhood today buys all its grapes and makes Labrusca and French hybrid table, fortified, and sparkling wines. Brotherhood and the Hudson Valley Wine Company of Highland are the two major Hudson Valley producers, who put out similar wines.

The really interesting Hudson River Valley wineries are the very small and often very new wineries. The original small Hudson Valley winery was High Tor, founded in 1949. High Tor was the first winery to produce exclusively French hybrids but now is closed, perhaps only temporarily.

The most interesting winery is Benmarl Wine Company at Marlboro. Founded by Mark Miller and his family in 1956, it produces French hybrids, both as varietals and jugs, and Chardonnay and Johannisberg Rieslings, the latter under the Cuvée de Vigneron label. The best wines probably are the Seyval Blanc and Baco Noir.

Benmarl developed an interesting cooperative idea. Several hundred supporters became members of the Benmarl Société des Vignerons. Membership entitled them to help out at the winery and to a number of bottles of wine each vintage. The winery now has a capacity of seventy-five thousand gallons, and the wines can be found in New York City and a few other locations. Expansion already underway will increase capacity to one hundred fifty thousand gallons. A third major producer is Great River Winery of Marlboro (sparkling and Labrusca and French hybrid table wines).

The Farm Winery Act has resulted in the establishment of several small wineries, the most interesting being Cottage Vineyards of Marlboro, which specializes in Johannisberg Riesling and Chardonnay; Cascade Mountain Vineyards, which specializes in producing wines that are ready to drink in the year of vintage; and Clinton Vineyards, which is growing Chardonnay and Johannisberg Riesling as well as white French hybrids, including an excellent Seyval Blanc.

The proximity of the Hudson Valley grapegrowing sections to New York City makes development of more small wineries inevitable. But none will appear so unexpectedly as did the lone Long Island vineyard, Hargrave Vineyards in Cutchogue.

The owners, Alexander and Louisa Hargrave, planted more than eighty acres to Cabernet Sauvignon, Pinot Noir, Sauvignon Blanc, Merlot, Johannisberg Riesling, and Chardonnay, and built their winery in 1973. All wines are estate-bottled and vintage-dated, and all that have been produced were much admired, particularly the Rosé of Cabernet Sauvignon. The first Cabernet Sauvignon was not released until 1978. Hargrave even has joined the trendy Californians who produce a Pinot Noir Blanc de Noir (*see* chapter 14).

The sea modifies temperatures in the North Fork district of Long Island, and grapes have long been grown there. The Hargraves think they have found a section of the country that will soon be much regarded. Their inclusion in an overview of the state exemplifies its diversity.

Despite the introduction of *Vitis vinifera* grapes to New York, it is likely that Gold Seal is right. Vinifera grapes can play a role in New York, but, except in the cases of specialist wineries, that role will always be small. The most exciting development in New York is the widespread conversion of old vineyards and the planting of new vineyards to French hybrid varieties. Native American grapes will never disapper. Nor should they. More "California wine" made outside California is hardly needed, and the growing appreciation for the unique qualities of French hybrid grapes will ensure that New York wines remain distinctive.

12

WINERIES OF THE OTHER STATES
Maryland to Missouri

The authoritative directory of U.S. wineries published by *Wines & Vines* magazine lists wineries in thirty-eight states. Thus far we have looked at California, Oregon, Washington, and New York and waved at, in passing, Colorado, Idaho, New Mexico, and Hawaii. It is a measure of the nature of the industry to survey the other thirty states in one chapter.

MARYLAND

Despite the fact that Maryland wine, which has a long history, is produced in only a handful of wineries from a few hundred acres, no account of the wine industry in the United States would be complete if it failed to cover Maryland.

Maryland's place is secure by being home to Philip and Jocelyn Wagner and their Boordy Vineyards, which they founded in 1942 in Riderwood, near Baltimore. The Wagner name has spotted this book, for good reason. Philip Wagner, a Baltimore newsman, in the 1930s established the first French hybrid vineyards in the United States.

Boordy produced its first vintage Baco Noir in the late 1940s, but long before then the Wagners had started campaigning on behalf of the hybrids, recommending them as substitutes for what they considered to be inferior Labruscas. The popularization of French hybrids was slow-going for many years, but as we have seen in the New York chapter, and as we will see in states as far apart as New Hampshire and Arkansas, the victory is as good as won. All hybrid growers and countless amateur and professional winemakers have been taught by Wagner's *American Wines and How to Make Them* (the latest edition, the fifth, is called simply *Grapes Into Wine*), and many vineyards have been started with stock acquired from the Wagners. For such a little winery, Boordy Vineyards has had an incalculable effect on the U.S. industry.

The essentially simple Boordy wines are hard to find. For a while after 1968, the name appeared on wines from three separate areas, made in the three distinct wineries. The tri-state venture failed, however. The Prosser, Washington, winery closed in 1976, and the Penn Yan, New York, endeavor came to an end in 1977. Today, Boordy Vineyards wines come, as usual, from the home vineyards near Baltimore.

Other wineries in Maryland include Montbray Wine Cellars, which produces both French hybrid and Vinifera wines, and Provenza Vineyards, which makes French hybrid blends.

PENNSYLVANIA

The Pennsylvania wine industry is significantly larger than Maryland's, with more than ten thousand acres of grapes under cultivation. There are about twenty working wineries, most coming into existence as a result of the Farm Winery Bill that became law in 1968.

Pennsylvania wineries are concentrated in the northwest, on the shores of Lake Erie, and in the southeast. The Lake Erie wineries, Mazza Vineyards, Penn-Shore Vineyards, and Presque Isle Wine Cellars, all belong in character to a belt of wineries that stretch along Lake Erie from Chautauqua to Ohio. Mazza and Presque Isle offer excellent French hybrids and Viniferas, including Cabernet Sauvignons. Penn-Shore is larger and more traditional, with an emphasis on Labruscas.

The oldest existing Pennsylvania winery is Conestoga Vineyards at Birchrunville (Labruscas and French hybrids in small quantities). Conestoga dates to 1963, but is now only one of many in the Philadelphia area. Others include the Adams County Winery, which has a strong commitment to Vinifera wines, growing many including Zinfandel; Buckingham Valley Vineyards in Bucks County; and Pequea Valley Vineyard, a popular tourist attraction in Willow Street.

OHIO

In northeast Ohio, associated with the Lake Erie vineyards of Pennsylvania and New York, are Markko Vineyard, Chalet Debonné Vineyards, Grand River Wine Company, and Cedar Hill Wine Company. Markko and Grand River produce estate-bottled Vinifera wines exclusively; their Chardonnay and Johannisberg Riesling are of remarkable quality. Chalet Debonné is a producer of Concord and French hybrid wines. Cedar Hill Wine Company, located in the cellar of the proprietor's Au Provence restaurant, makes wine under the Chateau Lagniappe label. The proprietor sells his wines only at the restaurant, but they are worth searching out. Both his French hybrids and Pinot Noirs have won prizes.

The real Ohio Lake Erie wineries are farther west. This is Labrusca country, both on the mainland around Sandusky and on the Lake Erie islands, though increasingly French hybrids are being introduced. The major producer has its winery in Cincinnati, not on the lakeshore. Meier's Wine Cellars, a 3.2-million-gallon operation, produces sparkling wines, especially its well-known Sparkling Catawba, and table wines. Meier's owns all of Isle Saint George, where it has seven hundred acres planted mostly to Labruscas and French hybrids, and Vinifera vineyards.

Other Sandusky-area wineries include Mantey Vineyards, which began as a Labrusca producer, added French hybrids, and now is growing some Vinifera; and Catawba Island Wine Company, owned by a brother of the owner of Mantey, which produces still table and sparkling wines under the Mon Ami label. Actually on the islands are Heineman Winery of Put-in-Bay and Leslie J. Bretz Winery of Middle Bass; both produce traditional Ohio Labrusca wines.

Most Ohio development is taking place in the south, near the Ohio River, where once Nicholas Longworth thought he had seen the future. The best-established of the wineries—there are several already in operation and more planned—are Tarula Farms in Clarksville and Valley Vineyards Farm in Morrow. Once again French hybrids are making the running in these new Ohio vineyards.

NEW JERSEY, NEW HAMPSHIRE, AND MASSACHUSETTS

Near Atlantic City, there are a number of wineries. The chief is Renault Winery of Egg Harbor City, producer of bulk-process sparkling wines made from Labrusca and California wine and the Labrusca varietal called Noah. Others include Gross' Highland Winery of Absecon and Tomasello Winery of Hammonton. The chief New Jersey winery makes wine not from grapes but from apples: Laird and Company, headquartered at Scobeyville.

New Hampshire boasts one winery, White Mountain Vineyards, in Laconia. White Mountain is a tribute to the enthusiam and skill of John and Lucille Canepa, who became convinced they could grow winegrapes in New Hampshire and set out to prove it. They grow French hybrid grapes and produce exceedingly popular wines, some blended with California wines. Their two labels are Canepa Estate-Bottled wines and Lakes Region wines.

In Massachusetts on Martha's Vineyard, an island off Cape Cod, is Chicama Vineyards, a thirty-acre, twelve-thousand-gallon winery specializing in Vinifera grapes. Chicama makes a very appealing Zinfandel from imported California grapes, but its own vineyards, planted with the advice of Konstantin Frank, are now coming in. The first wines, Chardonnay and Johannisberg Riesling, have been well received.

As more and more states adopt farm winery laws modeled on the one adopted by Pennsylvania in 1968, small wineries constantly spring up. Others will join Chicama in Massachusetts. Rhode Island and Connecticut already have some. White Mountain Vineyards in New Hampshire will have company. The effect of such laws is contagious. North Carolina now has several wineries, producing Muscadine wines for the most part. And states as far apart and as unfamiliar to wine enthusiasts as Kentucky and Mississippi have small wineries in operation.

Probably these will always be small ventures with devoted followings. The only other major group is a band of wine-producing states from Michigan in the North through Indiana to Missouri and Arkansas.

MICHIGAN

Michigan is a major producer of grapes, especially Labruscas, most of which are grown in the small section of southeast Michigan that borders Indiana.

Paw Paw is home of the state's largest winemaker, Warner Vineyards, with three million gallons' capacity; St. Julian Wine Company, half the size of Warner; and half-million-gallon Frontenac Vineyards. All three wineries are heavily planted to Labruscas, but Warner, in particular, is investing in French hybrids, with telling results.

Closer to Lake Michigan than Paw Paw is Keeler, the home of Bronte Champagne and Wines Company. Bronte has been growing hybrids for nearly thirty years and was one of the first wineries to label French hybrids varietally.

Its chief claim to fame is the invention of Cold Duck, a mixture of Labrusca sparkling wine and California Burgundy. Other people in Michigan dispute Bronte's claim, but it certainly put it on the market in 1964 and the wine had its genesis in Michigan.

The most interesting wineries in Michigan probably are Tabor Hill Vineyard, Fenn Valley Vineyards, and those in the Leelanau Penninsula.

Tabor Hill, a one-hundred-thousand-gallon winery, dates to 1970 and is located in Buchanan. Its owner, Leonard Olson, and his family produce only premium French hybrid and *Vitis vinifera* wines. When all the rest of Michigan scoffed, Tabor Hill demonstrated that Konstantin-Frank-type hardy-rooted Chardonnay and Johannisberg Rieslings will grow in Michigan. And its Chardonnays, aged in European oak cooperage, and Johannisberg Rieslings, especially the late harvest wines, are first rate.

Tabor Hill also produces very appealing dry Vidal Blanc, Seyval Blanc, Maréchal Foch, and Baco Noir French hybrid wines. Tabor Hill jugs, called Cuvée Blanc, Rouge, and Rosé, are cleanly made, dry, and very palatable.

Tabor Hill's pioneering has prompted imitation, in the form of Fenn Valley Vineyards, a winery of similar size. Tabor Hill buys some of its grapes. Fenn Valley plans to grow all its own, which include Gewürztraminer, but otherwise the two operations are similar.

The third new departure for Michigan is the development of Leelanau Peninsula, a couple of hundred miles north of the southeastern grape section of Michigan, in Grand Travers Bay. Chardonnay and Johannisberg Riesling are now thought to do well in this lake-tempered finger of land. Growers are putting in vineyards of Vinifera and French hybrids, and excitement runs deep. Several wineries are already bonded: Chateau Grand Travers (forty thousand gallons), Boskydel Vineyard (ninety thousand gallons), and Leelanau Wine Cellars (one hundred twenty thousand gallons). Others are planned, and this section of Michigan hopes to be known as a premium wine-producing area in a fairly short time.

For wines made in Wisconsin, the most interesting venture is The Wollersheim Winery outside Sauk City, which Agoston Haraszthy founded. What he failed to do over a hundred years ago, Robert and Jo Ann Wollersheim have succeeded in doing, chiefly with French hybrids. Wine is even made as far north as Minnesota; in Illinois at Thompson Winery near Chicago, which makes only sparkling wines; and at Nauvoo, on the Mississippi. Illinois actually is the third leading wine-producing state, but this ranking is due almost entirely to the huge Chicago Mogen David facility, which gets its grapes from outside the state—New York, Michigan, and Missouri, particularly.

INDIANA

In Indiana, there is a smattering of wineries. The major concentration is along the south shore of Lake Michigan, actually a continuation of the Michigan grape area.

The chief winery is the fifty-thousand-gallon Banholzer Winecellars of New Carlisle. Carl Benholzer originally was associated with Tabor Hill but has been in Indiana since 1974. Like Tabor Hill, Banholzer Winecellars is committed to French hybrids and *Vitis vinifera* grapes. But unlike Tabor Hill, Banholzer does not confine itself to Chardonnay and Johannisberg Riesling. In addition, it has planted Cabernet Sauvignon, Pinot Noir, and Gewürztraminer.

Indiana has its own "Pennsylvania" law, and as a result, a number of small wineries. Its other major wineries are Oliver Wine Company of Bloomington and Golden Rain Tree Winery of Wadesville. Both make French hybrid wines.

MISSOURI

Missouri was a very important wine state in the middle years of the nineteenth century, and its famous Cook's Imperial Champagne Cellar of St. Louis was known to all wine drinkers. But it suffered serious decline, which culminated in Prohibition. Recently, however, about twenty wineries have begun to make wines from Missouri grapes. Most produce Labrusca wines, though again French hybrids are increasingly to be found. Mount Pleasant Vineyards, founded in 1881, but long out of business, has been revived in its native Augusta and is producing French hybrids, Labrusca, and Johannisberg Riesling.

The largest winery in the state, Bardenheier's Wine Cellars of St. Louis, which for years was merely a bottler of out-of-state wines, now is growing and buying Missouri grapes.

Typical of the brand-new operations are Stone Hill Wine Company of Hermann and the Big Prairie wineries to the southwest of St. Louis: St. James Winery, Ziegler Winery, and Ozark Vineyards.

ARKANSAS

Missouri vineyards are largely planted to Concords. Many find their way to a Welch plant in Arkansas. Welch also buys Concords in Arkansas, also a significant producer of table and sparkling wines. The center of viticultural effort is the city of Altus, the home of the state's largest winery, Wiederkehr Wine Cellars, which dates to 1880.

Wiederkehr, with a capacity of over two million gallons, produces sparkling and table wines from Labrusca, French hybrid, and *Vitis vinifera* grapes. There are only a few of the latter, but all wines are exceptionally well made in a modern winery. They rank with premium wines of their types in other parts of the country.

There are three other wineries in Altus, and another half-dozen dot the state. But one has come to expect that. Wineries seem to be springing up everywhere—more than six hundred across the United States. We have mentioned in passing, or not at all, the wineries of Alabama, Colorado, Connecticut, Florida, Georgia, Hawaii, Idaho, Iowa, Kansas, Kentucky, Louisiana, Maine, Minnesota, Mississippi, New Mexico, North Carolina, Oklahoma, Rhode Island, South Carolina, Tennessee, Texas, and Wisconsin. Of those that have not been mentioned we can only advise: Go out and look for yourself.

Meantime, we can perhaps close this speedy national tour with Virginia. Virginia is the home of Canandaigua's Richard's Wild Irish Rose. It also has seen over the past ten years plantings of French hybrid and Vinifera vineyards. A handful of wineries have opened their doors.

Typical? It would seem so, except that in 1976 an Italian-British consortium began planting a two-hundred-fifty-acre vineyard of Vinifera in Barboursville. And in 1978 an equivalent-sized vineyard in Culpeper began to go in on behalf of a German interest.

Five hundred acres of Vinifera vines? In Virginia? If nothing else, the story of American wines is far from told. The future, in Virginia and across the country, will bear watching.

13

SPARKLING WINES
When Champagne Is Not Champagne

"Sparkling wine" and "champagne" are interchangeable terms in popular usage, and wineries producing sparkling wines are free to use the champagne label by law. Nonetheless, as with generic appellation, this practice is unfortunate. Just as real Chablis is a wine made of specified grapes grown in regulated ways and produced according to other regulations, real Champagne comes from a small section of France to the northeast of Paris, is made from certain specific grapes, and is produced under stringent supervision. In fact, probably no production and growing system is more tightly controlled than that of Champagne.

The purpose of all such systems is to ensure the integrity of the product, to make certain that no one debases the name common to all producers—Chablis or champagne or whatever—by foisting off as the named wine an inferior product and thereby bringing the whole industry into disrepute.

Given this sense of industry identification, one should not be surprised to learn that Champagne makers and the French government have frequently gone to court to prevent the use of the name by others—in France, other European countries, and outside Europe. Their argument, which has merit, is that wine not produced in the delimited Champagne area in the traditional, regulated manner cannot by definition be Champagne and, therefore, should not be passed off as "champagne."

Inside Europe, the assault on imitators has been entirely successful. For example, French sparkling wine produced outside Champagne is called *vin mousseux*. Outside Europe and especially in the United States the efforts have been largely rebuffed. Provided that they qualify the name with the state of origin—New York, California, Illinois—U.S. wineries may call any sort of wine with bubbles in it—that is, a wine that has undergone two fermentations—"champagne."

As with the use of generic labels, the ethics of this assumption are questionable. In addition, even inside the United States, where many forms of production technique are in use, to lump all bubbly wines into one category—champagne—is misleading. For these and other reasons, the term "sparkling wine" is used in this book.

French Champagne is made from Chardonnay, Pinot Blanc, and Pinot Noir—or the first two varietals alone—only, and the grapes must be grown in specified ways. After the wine has fermented, different wines are blended to make the *cuvée*, and the blend is placed in a bottle, from which it is never removed. A quantity of sugar and yeast is added. The bottle is sealed, and the second fermentation, the process that gives the wine its bubbles, takes place. At the end of the second fermentation, the wine is quite dry and the yeast cells inactive. Then the bottles are inserted by the neck into a board. Every few weeks, each bottle is given a quarter turn and slowly stood upright, top down. This riddling of the bottles gradually concentrates all the now-dead yeast cells in the neck of the bottle.

When the second fermentation and riddling processes are completed, the bottle neck is briefly frozen and the cap is removed. The gas in the bottle blows the now-frozen plug of yeast and other dead matter out. The bottle then is topped up with the *dosage*, a mixture of wine and wine sugar, and corked and labeled, ready for shipment.

This form of wine production is very expensive: The inventory is tied up for years, and the amount of hard work required is enormous. Even the bottles, which are specially designed to withstand the pressure of the gas in the wine, are expensive. Yet this *méthode champenoise* is the way all French Champagne is produced; it is also the way the best U.S. sparkling wines are produced.

More than sixty wineries in the United States make sparkling wine. Three—two in California, Gallo and United Vintners, and one in New York, Taylor Wine Company—produce more than five hundred thousand cases a year. Twenty-one wineries use the *méthode champenoise*, but of these only two, Korbel and Kornell, produce more than one hundred thousand cases a year. The vast majority produces fewer than five thousand cases a year. In other words, as one would expect, the *méthode champenoise* is not much used.

All sparkling wine undergoes two fermentations, but alternate methods, unacceptable in Champagne, have been invented to eliminate much of the increasingly costly handwork required by the *méthode champenoise*. The first process is called the *transfer process*.

Wineries using the transfer process follow the traditional methods through the secondary fermentation state. But then, the wine is poured out of the bottle under pressure into tanks, where the yeasts and other dead cells are filtered out. Finally, bottles are refilled with wine and the *dosage* is added as required. This process accomplishes the same result as the traditional method and, it is claimed, allows for more control over the wine's development. But it undoubtedly destroys much of the individuality of the bottled wine.

The final method is called the *bulk process*. The secondary fermentation takes place in bulk, in a tank, not in the bottle. In other words, both fermentations occur in tanks. When the secondary fermentation is complete, the filtered wine is bottled. This method is cheap and speedy. The resulting wine is generally so far removed from Champagne that comparison is fruitless.

All three methods are used in the United States. Fortunately the law requires that the appropriate method be identified. For wines produced by the *méthode champenoise*, the label will read "Fermented in *This* Bottle," and the bottle will be corked. Transfer method wines are labeled "Fermented in *The* Bottle." The bottle will have a cork *or* a plastic stopper. Bulk-process wines must use that term or the interchangeable "Charmat Process" on the label (the process was invented by a Frenchman named Charmat). The stoppers are almost always plastic.

The different production systems available explain some of the quality differences, which may be observed in the "bead," the bubble in the wine. Good-quality sparkling wine will exhibit a small bead, which will rise in a steady stream from the bottom of the glass and continue to rise for many minutes. Wine of less distinction is marked by larger bubbles, which soon disappear entirely.

Technical process is only one way in which sparkling wine producers can cut corners. We have seen that French Champagne must be made from Chardonnay, Pinot Blanc, and Pinot Noir grapes. No other varietal may be used. Not surprisingly these are three of the finest and most expensive varietals, which produce relatively little wine compared to heavy producers such as Thompson Seedless and Chenin Blanc.

In the United States any grape, in any combination, may be used for sparkling wine. The ubiquitous, bland Thompson Seedless is used in quantity by bulk-process producers. Better quality grapes, such as Chenin Blanc and French Colombard, also are much used, but only the very best producers make much use of such premium grapes as Chardonnay and Pinot Noir. Taylor, in New York, uses two Labruscas, Catawba and Delaware, and one French hybrid, Aurora, in combination to produce its popular sparkling wines.

A winery need not tell you the contents of its sparkling wine, but the label is not by any means valueless. It identifies the production process. It normally also tells you something about the relative sweetness of the wine and if it is vintage wine.

Sweetness is controlled by the *dosage*. When the secondary fermentation is complete, all sugar in the wine has been converted. The wine is quite dry. Thus when the *dosage* is added to the bottle (or tank), the winemaker may, at his choice, add either more dry wine or wine containing a measured amount of wine sugar. The final product usually will be labeled Natur, Brut, Extra Dry, or Demi-Sec, depending on the sugar level. As a rule, Natur wine is totally or almost totally dry; Brut contains about 0.5 percent sugar; Extra Dry, about 1.5 percent sugar; and Demi-Sec, which is quite sweet, about 4-5 percent sugar.

One drinks wine according to taste, but most of the cheaper, lesser-quality wines are made quite sweet, not just because Americans are thought to like wine on the sweet side but also because, as with any wine, sugars mask its basic quality—or lack of it. Bulk-process wines, therefore, are usually at least demi-sec sweet.

A vintage wine will be identified on the label, although the term has little meaning. All French Champagne is a blend of some sort—at least a blend of grapes and usually a blend of wines from different years. The skill of the Champagne winemaker lies particularly in his ability to blend different wines to produce a *cuvée* that complements the style his house is known for. Only in exceptional years will a vintage be proclaimed, and a vintage champagne is not necessarily better than a nonvintage champagne. It is merely more distinct, more individual.

In the United States the same applies. Sparkling wines are not respected for their varietal flavor, as is, for instance, a Chardonnay table wine. Sparkling wines are known for their style, or lack of it, for the degree to which they show quality in blending and vinification. That all, or even most, of the grapes did or did not come from a single vintage is largely irrelevant.

So far as taste or "style" is concerned, the best champagnes are elegant, refined wines. The best U.S. sparkling wines are fresh and fruity in comparison. The basic reason for this difference is, of course, the nature of the grapes used. Not only are the varietals used in France limited to three, while any grape may be used in the United States, but also the soil in Champagne is relatively poor and the climate cool. The vines have to "struggle" to produce quality grapes, and the richness of the grape is "earned," concentrated in the grape. In contrast, the soils of California are almost uniformly richer and the climate warmer, resulting in richer, "fatter" grapes.

The differences between the wines of France and of the United States are exaggerated by the use of different yeast strains during the second fermentation. The quality and identity of the component grapes *and* the time spent with the yeast after the second fermentation determine the quality of the wine. If it does not lie on the yeast for long, as with bulk-process-produced wine, the nature of the yeast is hardly an issue. But if, as with premium sparkling wine producers, it lies on the yeast for a considerable period, the nature of the yeast will affect the wine a great deal. If the strains differ, the wines will differ.

That brings us full circle. U.S. sparkling wines are not French Champagnes. Therefore, they are not Champagne, but they can be very satisfying, as a review of the industry indicates.

U.S. SPARKLING WINE PRODUCERS

The most interesting development in recent years in the U.S. sparkling wine industry is the 1973 establishment of Domaine Chandon in Yountville, in the southern part of Napa Valley. What makes Domaine Chandon noteworthy is the ownership and close supervision of Moet-Hennessy, a giant French conglomerate whose two stars are Hennessy brandy and Moet & Chandon Champagne. Moet and its subsidiaries are the world's largest and most successful champagne makers—its top-of-the-line Dom Perignon is probably the single most famous champagne. Its investment in Napa Valley, amounting to some $10 million, indicates how the French view the U.S. market and Napa as a resource area.

Domaine Chandon is totally committed to the traditional *méthode champenoise*. How could it be otherwise? Its winemaker is the cellarmaster of Moet in France. Only specified, traditional French Champagne grapes, though little Chardonnay, are used because Moet believes California grapes are too fruity. Its own yeast strains from Champagne have even been imported to make the wine as French in style as possible.

Domaine Chandon released its first wines in 1976, having used grapes grown by Trefethen Vineyards in Carneros, the coolest section of Napa. In 1977 the wines were distributed nationally. As Domaine Chandon's own vineyards produce fully and its very handsome operation reaches capacity, it expects to release about one hundred thousand cases every year.

Its two sparkling wines, Napa Valley Brut and Napa Valley Blanc de Noirs, are excellent additions to the U.S. scene. The Brut is a golden, fruity wine, showing no excessive yeastiness. The first two *cuvées* were two-thirds Pinot Noir and one-third Chardonnay, but Pinot Blanc may be added and the composition may change in other ways in the future. The Blanc de Noirs is a pale-salmon-colored, 100 percent Pinot Noir, charming and vital, having a long-lasting effervescence and an appealing fruitiness.

Domaine Chandon and its development—at the winery is one of the better Napa Valley restaurants, for example—have tended to overshadow some of the other top California producers. This is unfortunate, because several deserve as much attention as Domaine Chandon, maybe more since they started without the advantage of the Moet-Hennessy backing.

Perhaps the very best sparkling wines are those made by Schramsberg Vineyards, a small operation that first achieved recognition when its wines were served in the White House and carried by then President Richard Nixon on his first trip to China. No compromises are made at Schramsberg, which grows most of its own grapes—Chardonnay and Pinot Noir chiefly—makes its own wines in the traditional manner, and produces very little wine overall.

Situated in Calistoga, in northern Napa, Schramsberg produces as the top of its line a remarkable Blanc de Blancs Cuvée Reserve, a wine that has been held an extra period on the yeast. This wine, perhaps, comes closest in style to European elegance of any U.S. sparkling wine. Schramsberg's other wines include a regular Blanc de Blancs, a fruity and very popular blend of Chardonnay and Pinot Blanc; a Blanc de Noir, a more traditional sparkling wine in its gold color and fruitiness, which comes from Pinot Noir; and an unusual Cuvée de Gamay, a blend of Napa Gamay and Pinot Noir, pinkish in color and full-bodied in style.

The Schramsberg wines are all just short of being fully dry except for Crémant, which is demi-sec sweet and made from the Flora grape. It is closer to Asti Spumante, the Italian sparkling wine, than to the French-style wines of most of California.

The other leading Napa producers of sparkling wines are Heitz Wine Cellars, Beaulieu Vineyards, and Hanns Kornell Champagne Cellars. Heitz produces little sparkling wine. Beaulieu wines are heavily Chardonnay in composition and thus are quite fruity. Kornell, in comparison, uses Chardonnay very little. Its Sehr Trocke is quite dry and made largely from Johannisberg Riesling, a fact quite detectable in the aroma. The Kornell Brut, with a touch of sweetness, is less austere than other Bruts; it too is Riesling-based.

Neither Kornell nor Domaine Chandon uses vintage dating; both Beaulieu and Schramsberg do.

Count Haraszthy made one of the first California sparkling wines, so it is fitting that Sonoma be home to several *méthode champenoise* houses. They range from producers of small lots, such as Grand Cru, Château St. Jean, and Geyser Peak to those of large quantities, such as large Korbel. In between lies Sonoma Vineyards, which is unusual in that it uses oak-aged wines to make its *cuvée*.

Of all these, F. Korbel & Brothers is the most interesting. With an operation dating back more than one hundred years, Korbel has established a name for itself as the leading producer of generally available quality California sparkling wines. Its dry Natural is a blend of Chardonnay, Pinot Blanc, and Chenin Blanc. Its most popular wine, Brut, and its sweet Sec and Extra Dry are blends of Pinot Blanc, Chenin Blanc, French Colombard, and Burger. Korbel's most interesting wine is the 100 percent Pinot Noir Blanc de Noir. A pale pink, estate-bottled wine made from free-run juice, it is barely sweet and superbly finished.

Korbel has pioneered efforts to find ways to cut handwork, and therefore expense, involved in the traditional methods without sacrifice of quality. It has developed a motorized riddling rack and is experimenting with a refinement of the machine to riddle wines in cases, rather than individually.

Korbel's approach is to give the public a quality product at an agreeable price. Its wines are clean, acceptable, and very pleasant—not distinguished, but excellent values. Even though they may not reach levels of greatness, they have done much to educate U.S. consumers in the delights of well-made sparkling wine.

Away from Napa and Sonoma, the chief producer of *méthode champenoise* sparkling wine is Mirassou, which makes Monterey County wines—very fruity, distinctively varietal in character. Its quite dry Au Naturel and slightly sweet Brut exhibit their Monterey County origin, with its unique quality. Mirassou's "LD" wine has spent longer than customary on the yeast.

Mirassou and Korbel both make rosé sparkling wines, in both cases sweet. Mirassou's entry is Sparkling Gamay Beaujolais. Korbel has Rouge Champagne—Zinfandel, Pinot Noir, and Petite Sirah—and Rosé Champagne—Gamay and Zinfandel.

There are a few other traditionalists in California, but most sparkling wine is made by either the transfer or bulk-process method.

Among the transfer producers, Almadén should be singled out. Its Vintage Chardonnay Nature, Blanc de Blancs, and Eye of the Partridge (a golden-colored wine made largely from Pinot Noir) are first-rate examples of what can be done with the transfer method. Somewhat similar in style and quality are the Paul Masson entries: Brut and Extra Dry. Masson also makes a passably good, vintage sparkling wine from 100 percent Monterey County Johannisberg Riesling, a Pinnacles Selection wine.

It is said that if law allowed, French champagne makers would switch to the transfer method. The wines of Almadén and Masson suggest that much can be done with the process. The same cannot be said about the bulk (Charmat) process. Wines produced this way are almost without exception of little virtue. They are made usually of undistinguished grapes and rushed through what normally is a lengthy period of production. Only Christian Brothers produces wines of note by this process, and for the price that it charges decent transfer wines can be purchased.

At the very lowest end of the spectrum, the wines of such producers as André (Gallo) and Jacques Bonet (United Vintners) indicate that in sparkling wines, more than for most wines, you get what you pay for.

OTHER STATES

Sparkling wine is one of the few categories of wine production in which non-California states put up a good front, at least statistically. Whereas the other forty-nine states produce less than 10 percent (to California's more than 70 percent) of all table wines drunk in the United States, they produce close to 20 percent (to California's 70 percent) of all sparkling wines drunk.

In 1977, a *Vines and Wines* survey showed that sparkling wines are produced in California, Arkansas, Illinois, Michigan, Missouri, New Jersey, Ohio, Pennsylvania, and, particularly, New York.

The names outside New York are not well known except locally. Except for Warner Vineyards in Michigan and Meier's Wine Cellars in Ohio, none produced more than twenty-five thousand cases. Most, such as Thompson Winery (Père Marquete, Père Hennepin labels), produced less than five thousand cases. Each makes an interesting contribution, but not enough to justify further attention in this kind of survey.

New York is a different matter. Taylor Wine Company produces about 900,000 cases a year of Taylor and Great Western "champagnes." Monarch (Pol D'Argent and other labels) and Robin Fils (Gold Medal) produce more than 250,000 cases each. Canandaigua and Gold Seal produce between 100,000 and 250,000 cases each year, and several other wineries are active, too: Benmarl, Brotherhood, Bully Hill, Hudson Valley, Marlboro, Royal, and Widmer.

Most large sparkling wine producers concentrate on Labrusca and Labrusca/hybrid blends. New York State sparkling wine has a distinctive character relished by many—sweet and grapey—but its regular wine is largely undistinguished, except for its Labrusca woodiness.

The one large winery that does not fit this pattern is Gold Seal, primarily because of its extraordinary honorary president and former winemaker, Charles Fournier. A winemaker at Veuve Clicquot, one of the great names in French Champagne, Fournier arrived at Gold Seal in the early 1930s and quickly established Gold Seal's reputation for producing the best bottle-fermented transfer-process wines in the eastern United States. Many compare his Charles Fournier, Gold Seal, and Henri Marchant sparkling wines to the best produced in California.

Especially notable are the Charles Fournier Brut, made chiefly from Catawba. It has long been one of the best Gold Seal wines, though in recent years has ceded its place at the top of the Gold Seal list to the Charles Fournier Blanc de Blancs, made largely from Chardonnay grapes.

A measure of the success of Fournier and Gold Seal can be gauged by the wine event at the 1950 California state fair. Nineteen fifty was the first year non-California wines were allowed to enter the competition, and Gold Seal carried off the only gold medal. Since then non-California entries have again been barred.

Since we have defined U.S. "champagne" as sparkling wine, we could have also included Sparkling Burgundy, Cold Duck, and the plethora of sweet, fizzy wines that inundate the U.S. market from time to time. In fact, the most popular imported wine of the late 1970s, Lambrusco, is such a wine, coming from Italy.

But we need not spend more time on such products. The public tires of them rather quickly. Then they, or a close relation, appear in a slightly different guise and the cycle begins again. The fact that they are fad wines, with no staying power, is reason enough to dismiss them. Although "fun" to try when everyone is drinking them, they are so nondescript, in almost every case, they hold no interest beyond that of curiosity.

14

THE NEWEST WINES
Sweet Table Wines and White Red Wines

Nothing demonstrates more aptly the adaptability of the U.S. wine industry than the way it quickly seizes upon new trends and exploits them. Two of the newest are the production of late harvest sweet wines and dry white wines from red winegrapes. How this came about makes for a fascinating tale. The differences between the European and U.S. industries can hardly be more sharply defined than by comparing the lack of change in Europe with the rapid rate of change in the United States.

SWEET TABLE WINES

We have seen that the wine industry reacted to the chaos that descended at the end of Prohibition by devoting a large part of its energies to producing high-alcohol, very sweet, cheap wines.

By and large, the clientele for these wines had neither the money to buy more expensive wines nor any interest in them aside from getting drunk. For such a market, "dessert" wines were ideal. Unfortunately, so badly were the wines made and so unpleasant were the consequences of drinking them that the whole world of sweet wines was thrown into disrepute.

For people who like or might have liked quality sweet wines, the repercussions were both good and bad. On the one hand, many great imported sweet wines had to be underpriced in order to sell in the U.S., for example, those of Sauternes and Barsac—except Château d'Yquem, a first-growth Bordeaux. On the other hand, the U.S. industry steered clear of any involvement with wines that might be associated with the déclassé dessert wines of skid row.

In the last few years, this has changed, for several reasons. First, there is the discovery that Americans like their wines sweet, by and large. Second, the white wine boom brought into prominence the wines of Germany. Third, the natural inventiveness of winemakers, who, especially in small premium wineries, chafe against marketing restrictions, found a public response.

The first and third reasons are more or less givens. The second reason is worth comment, however. Unlike the wines of Sauternes and Barsac, which are made of Sémillon and Sauvignon Blanc, the great German wines are made of Johannisberg Riesling and are, consequently, all white. Furthermore, German vineyards along the Rhine and Moselle Rivers are so far to the north that their grapes never produce robust, strong wines. Instead, they produce light, flowery, fruity, sippable wines—the sort Amerians have discovered they like. All but the least-valued German wines are sweet. But in especially fortunate years the sugar content of some of the grapes reaches very impressive heights, and the resulting wines are extremely sweet, rather than just pleasantly sweet.

These very sweet wines are given the titles, in ascending order of sweetness, of *Auslese, Beerenauslese,* and *Trockenbeerenauslese.* Beneath the *Auslese* level is *Spätlese* and other lesser categories. What separates *Spätlese* from *Auslese* is a mold called *Botrytis Cinera*—"noble rot."

Botrytis is a fungus, a mold, that sometimes attacks grapes late in the year. It also can attack them earlier on, with disastrous results. Its effect is to shrivel the grape—it begins to look like a dirty raisin. As water is eliminated, grape sugars are concentrated, increasing in relation to the remainder of the grape.

These shriveled grapes produce relatively little grape juice, but the juice that materializes in the pressing is very sweet—sometimes more than 40 percent sugar as opposed to the average of less than 20 percent—and gives the wines the honey-sweet flavor botrytis imparts.

If their grapes are not hit by botrytis, Germans still make a pleasant sweet wine, whose style has been duplicated in California for many years. With botrytised grapes they make great wines, just as the French produce great sweet Bordeaux wines with grapes affected by the same mold.

The white wine boom led U.S. consumers to develop an appreciation for German wines. Most of the time, consumers drink lower grades of German wine, because they are more plentiful and reasonably priced than the higher. But the sweeter wines also have been discovered and appreciated, in the process putting an end to the canard about dessert wines fostered by the end of Prohibition.

This discovery was matched by an even more important development: Botrytis was discovered in California. Probably it had been there all along but had gone unrecognized. In any case, it is now found everywhere. Indeed, the mold has become such a commonly encountered phenomenon that one may well suspect overenthusiastic seekers are sometimes inclined to find it where it does not exist.

Sweet Rieslings have been available as long as the vine has been grown in California, but since the California climate is so encouraging to growth, the grapes tend to be fatter and less acidic than those produced in Germany. Rieslings tend often to lack balance and to be flat and cloying. In consequence, most of the time Rieslings are fermented dry. The blandness of California Rieslings is still encountered in late harvest wines, but botrytis tends to concentrate flavors as well as sugars, somehow overcoming the tendency to cloyingness in a well-made wine.

As the trickle of sweet wines has reached practically flood proportions, nomenclature has proved to be quite a problem. To begin with, wineries called their wines almost anything, including *Spätlese* and *Auslese*, which is what Wente Brothers called theirs. Now, however, BATF insists the wines be labeled "late harvest," which is not a very useful term, since it means very little. The label must show the sugar content at picking time and the residual sugar in the wine after fermentation, which is a more useful description.

Finally, a word of warning, which is underlined by the sugar readings on the labels: Botrytis affects grapes *individually*. A vineyard may be affected in such a slight manner at picking time that the botrytis contribution is negligible. Conversely, a heavily affected vineyard will exhibit very strong botrytis flavor. In Germany, the greatest wines, the *Trockenbeerenauslesen*, are picked grape by grape, literally. In the United States individual grape picking seldom occurs. This is where sugar readings on the label should help one make the right decision.

These wines are expensive for the most part. They should be, since relatively little wine is made from late harvest grapes. However, not *all* the wines are expensive nor will *only* heavily botrytised grapes produce good quality wines. In 1975 Almadén made considerable quantities of a very appealing late harvest wine. Many wines now sold as late harvest are extremely attractive without being truly memorable.

The Wines

The pioneer in sweet table wine production was Myron Nightingale, now with Beringer. In the late 1950s, Nightingale introduced botrytis artificaially into Sémillon and Sauvignon Blanc grapes while he was with Cresta Blanca, then in Livermore Valley. The resulting wine, called Premier Sémillon and first issued in 1961, was remarkable, but it was soon decided that the process was too difficult and expensive to undertake to make the effort worthwhile on a continuing basis.

Wente Brothers began to produce its series of *Spätlese* and *Auslese* wines from Monterey County grapes in 1969. Others made instructive efforts, and then the floodgates opened with the introduction of the 1973 Freemark Abbey Edelwein. So highly regarded and much celebrated was this wine that winery operators finally and fully concluded that botrytis did exist, that salable wines could be made from botrytised grapes, and, perhaps most important, that consumers would pay the necessary prices for such wines.

Since 1973 the acceleration of production has been acute, though while many such wines are on the market, with more on the way, the quantity of each is severely limited. As we have seen, botrytis decreases yield and is only exceptionally encountered in any case.

An example of the range of production is that of Freemark Abbey in 1976, when it produced three late harvest Rieslings. Its Sweet Select Riesling had a 3.3 residual sugar reading, roughly equivalent to an *Auslese*. Its Edelwein reached 12.4 and, like the 1973, equaled a

Beerenauslese wine. Its Edelwein Gold reached a remarkable 16.4 sugar reading and qualified as a *Trockenbeerenauslese*.

It is not hard to make sweet wines, but difficult to make non-cloying, light sweet wines exhibiting a great deal of fruitiness and balanced by sufficient acid. Yet that is exactly what many California wineries are doing, usually at a low-alcohol level.

Other examples of success in this area are Burgess Cellars and Chateau St. Jean. At the latter, winemaker Dick Arrowood in 1977 produced Rieslings with sugar readings ranging from 1.60 (*Kabinett*-style) to 25 (*Trockenbeerenauslese*) with an 18 (*Beerenauslese*) and a 4.8 (*Auslese*) thrown in for good measure. In a 1978 New York tasting, Chateau St. Jean wines swept all honors in competition with some highly regarded German wines.

The great wines of Chateau St. Jean and Freemark Abbey are very expensive. So are those of Joseph Phelps Vineyard, where an impressive array of late harvest Rieslings are being made, up to and including the *Trockenbeerenauslese* level (reached in 1976) and *Beerenauslese* level (1975, 1976, and 1977). Less expensive but still very well made is The Monterey Vineyard 1977 Thanksgiving Harvest Johannisberg Riesling, which has a residual sugar reading of 5.4 (*Auslese*).

A winery making great strides these days is San Martin, having equipped itself fully to handle small batches of grapes in the most modern way. In 1976 and 1977 it produced Santa Clara late harvest Johannisberg Rieslings that were truly remarkable because they retailed for around $5 and yet were very well in balance with a 7.8 sugar reading (*Auslese*).

Other wineries that have achieved considerable success with late harvest Rieslings include Chateau Montelena, Caymus, Veedercrest, Stag's Leap Wine Cellars, Sonoma Vineyards, and Beringer, as well as such small wineries as Hacienda, Hop Kiln, Field Stone, and J. Lohr. The success of The Firestone Vineyard, which produced a superb late harvest Johannisberg Riesling in 1976, indicates that botrytis can be found in most parts of California.

Johannisberg Rieslings produce most of the best late harvest California wines. However, botrytis attacks most kinds of white grapes, and late harvest wines are being made from other varietals.

For example, in Monterey County, The Monterey Vineyard has made a botrytised Sauvignon Blanc (with some Sémillon), a wine not unlike a Sauterne except that it has the minty flavor of Monterey. Also in Monterey, Paul Masson makes a botrytised Gewürztraminer, its Pinnacles Selection. In Santa Clara Valley, San Martin made a 1977 Sémillon with an 8 reading, well made, clean wine at an appealing retail price.

The experience of Callaway Vineyard in Rancho California reinforces that of Firestone with respect to the existence of botrytis in southern California. One of Callaway's first wines was a first-rate late harvest Chenin Blanc, labeled Sweet Nancy after the winemaker's wife. In 1975 the Sweet Nancy residual sugar reading was 7 percent. Callaway also produced an outstanding, very expensive late harvest Johannisberg Riesling, which is one of the best of its kind.

Other late harvest Chenin Blancs have been produced by Sterling, which calls its wine Chenin D'Or, and Bargetto.

Another varietal successfully produced in the late harvest manner is Gewürztraminer. The Paul Masson Monterey wine has been mentioned already. Perhaps more typical of the varietal are the wines of Chateau St. Jean and Hacienda in Sonoma and of Veedercrest and Joseph Phelps in Napa.

The list is almost endless, and the wines are not confined to California. Tabor Hill in Michigan, for example, makes a very appealing late harvest Johannisberg Riesling, and several eastern winemakers have done the same, notably Konstantin Frank.

It is clear that great progress has been made. Even though the lack of acid in many California grapes means that late harvest wines will not in all cases taste as sprightly as their German cousins, many now available are of very good quality. Moreover, the trend is unmistakable: We will see more and more late harvest whites. That they are sometimes less than perfect is far less important than that they can be very fine indeed and have destroyed the antipathy toward "dessert" wines that existed for so many years.

WHITE WINES FROM RED GRAPES

What does one do when the world demands white wines and one has an overabundance of red-wine-producing grapes? Especially when many of those grapes are a relatively unpopular varietal? Make white wine, of course. Specifically make white wine from Pinot Noir.

In 1974 there were almost four thousand acres of Pinot Noir planted and bearing in California. By 1977 a further six thousand acres had come into production, and growers found they had a surplus on their hands. Much excess tonnage is now used for jug wines (chapter 5), but canny winemakers have also discovered that, with care, they can make acceptable and even quite decent white wines from red Pinot Noir grapes.

All grape juice is virtually colorless. The skins of the grapes give color to the wines. As Champagne makers long ago discovered, if you press Pinot Noir grapes quickly, and immediately rack the wine off the skins, the red pigments in the skins do not contaminate the juice.

Champagne makers enjoy the advantage of picking their Pinot Noir grapes relatively early, when the sugar value is low and the acidity high. They want light wines, and their still white wines, called Côteaux Champenois, are perfect examples of the sort of wine they would produce at all times if they did not make Champagne: delicate, very dry, acidic, light-bodied.

When one picks Pinot Noir later, the wines are fuller and heavier-bodied, therefore more apppealing as table wines. But when Pinot Noir is picked at the peak of ripeness, it is virtually impossible to separate the juice and skins quickly enough to prevent the juice from picking up a tinge of color.

It took the surge of demand for white wines to get wineries to run the risk of rejection of white wines produced from Pinot Noir, but once it was discovered that the public found them acceptable, the initial hesitancy disappeared. By 1977 white Pinot Noirs were, like late harvest wines, the newest thing in California.

The first thing to note is that they are not "white" in the sense a Chardonnay or Chenin Blanc is. They almost all have a salmon-pink tinge of greater or lesser intensity.

What does one call them? Like late harvest wines, there is confusion about the correct term. The obvious choice is Blanc de Pinot Noir or Pinot Noir Blanc, but in fact many names are used.

The Wines

The first to use Pinot Noir for white wines in California was Caymus, which has made one every year since 1972 with great success. Caymus now calls its wine Oeil de Perdrix—Eye of the Partridge—as a tribute to its coppery color.

Bird eyes, in fact, are a popular form of nomenclature. Sebastiani has an Eye of the Swan, a Pinot Noir Blanc it introduced in 1975. Since Sebastiani is such a successful winery, its production of this wine was noted in many quarters, with a resulting increase in the entries of Pinot Noir Blanc.

By the end of 1977 about a dozen wineries had begun to produce white wines from Pinot Noir grapes. Caymus, Joseph Phelps, and Rutherford Hill, all Napa wineries, produce intense, full wines. Others follow the trend of the champagne makers, producing a lighter wine, quieter and more acidic in nature. It is not surprising that this group is headed by Domaine Chandon, which produces a Fred's Friends Pinot Noir Blanc, and Chateau St. Jean (Blanc de Noir), both of which make sparkling wine from Pinot Noir. Almadén, it will be recalled from chapter 13, produces a sparkling Pinot Noir called Eye of the Partridge. These three are joined by such wineries as Grand Cru, Franciscan, Geyser Peck, and Kenwood.

Another major producer, Wente Brothers, entered the lists in 1977. Undoubtedly there will be others in the future, and one can look forward to interesting experiments.

Some experimentation also is occurring with other varietals. We have seen how Pinot Noir is being used for rosé as well as white wine. The same is happening with Zinfandel and even the king of the reds, Cabernet Sauvignon. David Bruce and Montevina were two of the first to produce a "white red" using Zinfandel. Their example has been followed by other wineries such as Sutter Home. Pedrizzetti has even brought out a white Barbera, Barbera-Bianca.

Such wineries as Montevina and Fetzer make white Cabernet Sauvignons—free of tannin, of course. The tannin comes from the skins, stalks, and pits, all of which are separated from the juice as soon as possible. But even without tannin, the wines of Montevina make clear that white Cabernet Sauvignons can be agreeable. White Cabernet Sauvignons are probably curiosities, to be treated as such. It is unlikely they will be around much or long, since the demand for Cabernet Sauvignon for red wine is constant. However, there is little doubt that white Pinot Noirs and some white Zinfandels will be produced for the indefinite future. The public has put its seal of approval on these wines by buying them, and wineries will continue to be faced by the demand for white wines and an oversupply of Pinot Noir. The conclusion is inevitable.

15

THE HEAVY HITTERS
Port, Sherry, and Brandy

Even casual readers of this book will have detected a bias against "fortified" or "dessert" wines. At one time such wines accounted for about 75 percent of U.S. production, and in general they are best described by the epithet Sneaky Pete. Sold by the pint or half-pint they are sweet, heavy, alcoholic, and liable to make drinkers think they've been kicked in the head.

This chapter is written to set the record straight to some degree. Dessert wines are usually a product of grapes of the Muscat family—hence the generic name Muscatel. They give the category a bad name, but there are variations on this theme that deserve some attention.

In this category one could include the whole family of vermouths, the aromatics—fortified wines into which nonwine taste essences, herbs, fruit flavors, and the like have been blended. Dry vermouth is flavored with wormwood, for example. A fruity version is Ripple. Most such wines have relatively short lives; Thunderbird, a Gallo product, is one of the longest lasting. They are introduced and abandoned according to a reading of the market. Such wines are also less "winelike" than the chief fortified wines, port and sherry, which are the only two categories we will discuss.

Before we do so, however, we should make clear what the term *fortified* means. Fortified wines usually are sweet; if they are dry, or dryish, they often are called apéritif wines. In either case, they are made of fermented grape juice to which a wine distillate, brandy, is added. The yeasts necessary to convert sugar to alcohol die when the alcohol level of the mixture reaches 14 percent, which is the reason most fortified wines are sweet. By law, fortified wines are defined as wines having an alcoholic level of 14-21 percent.

The admixture of the brandy with its alcohol makes the wines very stable—a problem with very sweet grapes that produce little acid to balance their sugars—the sort of grapes, in other words, grown in hot climates. The first fortified wines were those of Spain (Sherry), Portugal (Port), and Italy (Marsala). In the hot climates these countries customarily experience, grapes become very ripe, very sugary, and very bland. The wines produced are therefore uninteresting and unstable. Fortifying them with brandy, it was found, gave them stability and permitted the development of techniques to give them character.

PORT

Port—or *porto*, as the Portuguese call it, to distinguish it from U.S.-made Port—was an invention of English merchants, whose cold-blooded compatriots, shivering in their winter cold and damp, took solace in glasses of the heavy, sweet wine. Today, most of the great names in Portuguese port still are British.

The classic Port production techniques involve, among other steps, the selection of grapes of certain varieties; cool fermentation, to insure that the fruit of the grape does not become lost; the addition of high-proof brandy to stop fermentation at a predetermined sugar level; and the aging of the wine in casks or, for true vintage Port, in bottles. A small amount of white Port is made, but the vast majority of Port is red.

These steps are followed to some degree by all U.S. Port makers. Most producers of this generic-type wine are in the San Joaquin Valley in central California, though many carry the names of producers associated with Napa (Christian Brothers and Beringer), Sonoma (Sebastiani and Buena Vista), Santa Clara (Paul Masson and Almadén), or other locations.

The differences in production lie chiefy in the beginning and end steps. First, U.S. regulations allow the use of any type of grapes at all, although most U.S. ports are made from specified grape varieties, only two of which—Souzo, used in Portugal and the United States mostly for color, and Tinta—are much found in the United States. If you do not use the same grapes, the wines can never be the same, though the University of California developed Rubired specifically for use in Port and there are some twelve thousand acres of this variety.

Second, few U.S. producers age their Ports in the classic manner. There are vintage ports in the United States—that is, wines produced from the grapes of one vintage as defined by BATF regulations—but these wines are released far too soon by Portuguese standards and are not aged in the bottle as true vintage Port must be. The other Portuguese categories, Late Bottled Port, Tawny Port, and even Ruby Port, have spent years—often many years—in barrels, aging and maturing.

The aging process is very expensive. First, inventory is tied up for years. Second, there is a loss, through evaporation, of something like 2 percent of the volume per year. A Portuguese Tawny, aged properly, will lose close to 20 percent of its initial volume before it is bottled.

In these circumstances, U.S. nomenclature is virtually meaningless. Though one comes across terms such as Rare Solera Cask, Rich

Ruby, Vintage Tawny, and many other variations, realistically California Port is California Ruby Port—seldom more, often less.

U.S. Ports, and certainly almost all non-California Ports, are usually less fine than a decent Portuguese Ruby when they cost less than $2.00. Between $2.00 and $3.00, the choice is wide, and some of the better choices are Novitiate Tinta, Cresta Blanca Souzo Ruby, Paul Masson Tawny, and Sebastiani Adagio Tawny.

At the top of the ladder are such wines as the traditional favorite, Ficklin Tinta; J. W. Morris Port Works Founder's; Parducci Tawny; Paul Masson Rare Souzo.

Ficklin Vineyards, which makes much use of traditional Port winegrapes and has had a *solera* since 1948, has long been regarded as the producer of the best U.S. Ports. But it is being challenged by J. W. Morris Port Works of Emeryville, Alameda County, which uses late harvest Pinot Noir and Ruby Cabernet grapes to make its port. Since it has only recently gone into production, its wines are very difficult to find. Nonetheless, the appearance of this label is most encouraging. Parducci's very agreeable, but expensive, Tawny is nearly as hard to find. East-Side's Tawny is widely available and is of some note.

Often unfairly overlooked is the Paul Masson operation. Masson's Tawny has been mentioned. Its Rare Souzo is made of 100 percent Souzo wines and aged for at least five years. The result is a California Port of exceptional quality.

Finally, another new producer, QuadyWinery, of Madera, makes an appealing Zinfandel port, but only in small quantities.

SHERRY

The British have had as much a hand in the development of the Spanish Sherry industry as in the Portuguese Port industry. In fact, the word "Sherry" is an anglicization of the Spanish "Jerez," the town in southern Spain that is the center of sherry production.

Like Port, Sherry is fortified with brandy, but in this case the brandy is added when the fermentation is over and the wine is totally dry. All sherries are quite dry, though some—the *olorosos*— seem sweeter because they are fuller than the others—the *finos*. At a late stage selected *olorosos* are sweetened and called cream, milk, golden, or just sweet Sherry.

All Spanish Sherry passes through the *solera* aging system. A *solera* is a system of barrels, stacked row upon row. The youngest wines are stacked at the top, the oldest at the bottom. As they age, wine is drawn off from the lowest barrels to be bottled and shipped. However, the lowest barrel is never emptied; seldom is more than one-tenth drawn off in any one year. Then it is topped up with wine from the barrel above it, which is in turn topped up with wine from the barrel above it. And so on.

Thus, the wine in the lowest barrel is a blend of the wine in *all* the barrels above. This is why there is no vintage wine, and also why Sherry is aged about ten years.

The system was developed when it was discovered that an older wine imparts its character to newer wines added to it. It is this double maturing process—of age in barrels, and mixing younger wines and older wines—that gives Sherry its very special character.

This process is, like that involved in the production of Port, slow and costly, for the same reasons. The wines produced, though, are the real thing.

In the United States, "Sherry" and "Port" are generic labels. So long as the alcohol levels conform to the BATF regulations, the winemaker can use whatever process he likes to produce them.

Most wineries start off on the wrong foot altogether. In Spain, Palomino makes up about 90 percent of the grapes used for Sherry. In the United States, grapes are used at will, though there are four thousand acres of Palomino in California. In the East, Concord, Dutchess, and other Labrusca grapes are used.

Having picked "wrong" grapes, most U.S. wineries use "wrong" technology. Most U.S. Sherries are "baked"; that is, the fortified wine, its fermentation arrested, is heated to well over 100 degrees Fahrenheit and maintained at that temperature for several months. It is then cooled and bottled. The finished wine has a popular, flat taste. A few wineries—notably Almadén, Louis Martini, Sebastiani, Llords & Elwood, and San Martin in California; Taylor and Widmer in New York—have established *soleras*, but even these wineries do not produce all their Sherries by means of the *solera* system.

A characteristic of all Spanish *fino* Sherries is the development of *flor* on the wine. *Flor* is a yeast that grows on the surface of the wine and imparts it with its typical yeasty flavor. When U.S. Sherries are baked, *flor* cannot develop. Companies such as Cresta Blanca have experimented with a "submerged-*flor*" process, with agreeable results. The fact remains, however, that the U.S. consumer likes the baked taste of U.S. Sherries, so the baking method is far and away the most used.

U.S. Sherries are sold as dry, cocktail, or pale Sherries (less than 2 percent sugar), as medium Sherry or simply as Sherry (2-4 percent sugar), and as sweet, cream, or mellow Sherry (more than 4 percent sugar). When *flor* has been used in the production, it is usually indicated on the label. One of the better *flor* varieties is Concannon's Prelude.

Other producers whose Sherries can generally be relied upon include Almadén, which has the longest-established *solera*, Bargetto, Beaulieu, Christian Brothers, Cresta Blanca, East-side, Gemello, Inglenook, Llords & Elwood, Richert, San Martin, Sebastiani, Taylor, and Widmer.

U.S.-produced Port and Sherry must, according to BATF regulations, carry notice of its derivation on the label: *New York* Sherry, *California* Port, etc. Conversely, imported Port is called *Porto* on the label, and imported Sherry is called *Spanish* Sherry. There is no reason for confusion of choice. There almost certainly will be no confusion in terms of taste.

BRANDY

In some ways, one should perhaps deal with brandy before writing about Port or Sherry. Both of the latter require the use of brandy at some point in the production process. Moreover, people have been distilling wine into brandy for practically as long as they have been fermenting grape juice into wine. On the other hand, since brandy —distilled wine—is one step further away from the beverage most of this book is concerned with, it seems appropriate to keep it to the end.

Brandy production involves the use of a relatively simple technology. Wine is heated by steam in a still—simply a closed container—until the liquid evaporates. The gases given off are collected and cooled. The liquid that forms is brandy.

This liquid is highly alcoholic, having a proof value of 150-170 (75 to 85 percent alcohol), colorless, and virtually undrinkable. The next step, therefore, is to cut the alcohol by the addition of distilled water, until it is about 100 proof. Then it must be aged in barrels. Barrel aging is the process that gives the brandy color and taste, though the former may be "improved" by the addition of a tasteless caramel. By U.S. law brandies must be aged at least two years in the wood, and many are aged for eight years or even longer.

Finally, the liquid is cut with water again, so that it falls to about 80 proof, and bottled, ready for shipment and consumption.

Unlike the situation with Sherry and Port, there is no "platonic" brandy—an ideal on which imitations are based or modeled. The most famous brandy of all is French and is called Cognac. Another French brandy of almost equal fame is Armagnac.

Thus, except to aid in description, it is unfair to compare U.S. brandies with European ones, especially since brandy production has a long tradition of its own in the United States.

When the Franciscans began to build their chain of California missions, they introduced not only the Mission grape but also brandy distillation processes. In 1769 vineyards were planted at Mission San Diego for the cultivation of vines for production of grapes and brandy. In short order, Mission San Fernando became noted for brandy production.

Jean-Louis Vignes began to produce brandy in Los Angeles in the 1830s, and Count Agoston Haraszthy and General Vallejo were making it in Sonoma as soon as they were producing wine.

In this century, brandy production has been confined entirely to the San Joaquin Valley and is centered in Lodi. Today about two hundred different brandies are produced, though some twenty-five producers make about 90 percent of U.S. brandy. U.S. brandy accounts for around 80 percent of all brandy consumed in the United States.

The French operation in Cognac is geared to producing brandy with a very distinctive character. Cognac, in comparison with U.S. brandies, is much heavier, much sharper on the palate—a characteristic imparted by pot-still distillation. While pot stills are to be found in California, their brandies are used mostly for blending. The most common production process there is the continuous still, which produces a lighter and more rounded brandy than the pot still. When it is finished in American oak barrels, this is the brandy preferred by the U.S. consumer. To a person accustomed to Cognacs, the taste is somewhat flat; it certainly has less bite.

American brandy is made mostly from Flame Tokay and Thompson Seedless grapes, whose quiet and unspectacular nature is exactly what brandymakers look for. Their aging process takes place in American oak barrels, which are almost always charred or used for other wine purposes before brandy aging. Through such means the effect of the oak on the brandy is ameliorated. The aim constantly is to produce a light, nontannic wine, quite the opposite of the French style.

Brandy is almost never a vintage wine. Given the distillation of the base wine and then the flavoring of the distillate as a result of contact with the wood, the skill of the brandymaster lies chiefly in his ability to blend individual brandies in different barrels, each of which would on its own produce a different-flavored brandy, so that the final blend fits the winery's image. This does not mean that vintage brandy is not produced; it is merely an exception. In 1966, for example, Cresta Blanca made a 95 percent Flame Tokay vintage brandy that shows very well and is priced most reasonably.

The largest and most respected producer of brandy is Christian Brothers, whose plant at Mount Tivy Winery in Reedley, California, dates back to 1884, though Christian Brothers have owned it only since the end of World War II. Mount Tivy's thirteen-million-gallon storage and aging plant makes it the producer of about one-third of all brandy produced in the United States.

The regular Christian Brothers blend, composed of pot- and continuous-still brandies, is a mild, quiet brandy with a muted nose. Its top-of-the-line brandy, Christian Brothers XO Rare Reserve Brandy, is, in contrast, nearly deserving of the fanfare that accompanied its 1972 introduction. At least 50 percent of XO Rare Reserve is composed of eight-year-old pot-still brandies, which explains its high price. XO Rare Reserve is the best U.S. brandy, though Guild's Ceremony brandies, eight and five years old, run close.

Less appealing brandies by comparison, but still showing considerable breeding and individuality, are United Vintners' Lejon, made at Madera at the huge Mission Bell complex, Schenley's Coronet VSQ, Setrakian, Beaulieu, Korbel, Paul Masson, and California Wine Association's A. R. Morrow Aristocrat.

16

VINTAGES
Storing, Serving, and Drinking Wine

Everyone at all familiar with wine knows something about vintage dating, the custom of printing on the wine label or neck label the year in which the grapes used to make the wine were picked. Virtually everyone has experienced at some point a sinking feeling when confronted with an unfamiliar wine list—the feeling of helplessness that sweeps over one when everything learned and carefully committed to memory suddenly blanks out. Was 1972 a good year in Bordeaux or Burgundy—or both? Choose wrong and you risk spending money unwisely and incurring the silent ridicule of the wine steward and more knowledgeable table companions.

Does it really matter? Well, yes and no, as we shall see. In any case, given the almost mystical significance accorded a vintage date, consideration of the vintage factor in terms of U.S. wines has been conspicuous by its absence from this book.

The lack of attention is not an oversight. Rather, the vintage date is of less importance, relatively speaking, for most U.S. wines than for most imported wines.

Some say that vintages are not important anyway, and they are partly right. But vintages and their listed dates on wine bottles tell us some things of importance, as does the absence of such dates. And to place their role in perspective, one first must look at why they have received such prominence, which means reviewing the European situation.

Most European wine never leaves Europe—in fact, most never leaves the locality of its production. The *vin ordinaire* of France and its equivalent all over Europe is a simple, blended, not very good wine—or rather, many simple, blended, not very good wines—that is produced and sold as soon after the grape harvest as possible, and drunk up by the time the next year's wine is ready to replace it on the market. Nobody pays it any more attention than one would pay to a can of soda.

It is economic to import only Europe's better wines, which in total are not in great supply. In France, for example, only about one-sixth of the production is given the top quality ranking *Appelation D'Origine Contrôlée(AOC), and only some of that reaches the United States. Wine of the second rank, entitled to the Vins Délimités de Qualité Supérieure* (VDQS) rating, is almost never seen in the United States. The same can be said for Germany and, increasingly, Italy, Spain, and elsewhere. (The ratings and regulations differ for each country, of course.)

In other words, imported wines usually are some of the best that a particular industry produces. This claim to quality is matched by the prices charged: the better the wine, the more one is expected to pay. This is where vintage considerations become important. If you are going to pay a premium price, you want to be sure you are getting wine of a quality that justifies it.

Premium wines from Europe are produced from grapes of one vintage if they show a vintage date. There have been scandals regarding misrepresentation in the past, but the date is more and more to be trusted. If the weather was bad during one particular growing season, all the winemaker's skills can make the wines only acceptable. They can never produce as fine a wine as one made in a good year. A less skillful, or more unlucky, winemaker will not even make the wine palatable.

To illustrate the importance of this condition, let us return to the dilemma expressed at the beginning of the chapter. Nineteen seventy-two was generally a disastrous year in Bordeaux, and a person looking at a totally unfamiliar list in a restaurant would do well to stay away from the 1972 offerings. Conversely, 1972 was a fairly successful year in Burgundy, especially for red wines, and the selection of a 1972 Burgundy would be a promising choice.

This rather long preamble explains how vintage dates have earned their reputation. By inference, it also explains why U.S. wine vintages play less of a role than the vintages of imported European wines.

In the first place, the bulk of the wines produced and drunk in the United States matches the *vin ordinaire* of France in concept. In quality, as we have seen, they are better generally. The jug wines discussed in chapter 5, the sparkling wines of chapter 13, the fortified wines of chapter 15, and the lesser wines of all U.S. wineries are blends, almost without exception, made to be marketed successfully—to be pleasant wines, no more. By definition, in these wines vintage differences, especially vintage weaknesses, are blended out by winemakers. Moreover, those simple wines made of blends of different vintages may carry no vintage date. Consumers simply require that they not vary in taste from one bottle or year-of-purchase to the next.

Most consumers drink these wines most of the time, and clearly the vintage date can mean virtually nothing. At the most, the consumer could use it as a guide to how old the wine is, since all such wines should be drunk young.

The role of the vintage in California is not even so important as in France and Germany with the majority of wines on which it *is* listed, for two reasons. (So little non-California vintage-dated wine is produced that it can be altogether ignored in this discussion.)

The first reason lies in the steadiness of California's weather. Since the climate is so propitious, it is easier to make premium wine in California in general than in France and Germany, so there are virtually no disastrous years and, conversely, fewer truly magnificient vintages. The terrible Bordeaux vintage of 1968 is unlikely to be encountered in California. Likewise, the magnificence of the 1976 Rhine vintage is less likely to occur. The unlikely does happen, of course. The 1968, 1970, and 1974 California vintages are noteworthy. A knowledge of European vintage characteristics is vital to ensure one chooses the best available wine. That is the positive side. The negative, but equally important, side is that such knowledge keeps the consumer from being especially disappointed in a purchase. Due to the excellence of California's climate, neither of these conditions ever applies to the degree they both do in France and Germany. You can be disappointed in a California wine, but generally the reason does not lie in the failure of the complete vintage.

The second reason is the nature of most California wines. Most inexpensive U.S. wines, as we have seen, are blends, but so are wines that are labeled varietally. There are very few 100 percent Pinot Noirs about, for example. Even those that are 100 percent will in all probability be composed of grapes grown in different parts of a specified region. They may come from many parts of one section— Napa, for example—or one area—North Coast Counties—or even one state—California. Even a winemaker producing a 100 percent Napa Valley Pinot Noir has great latitude in making his wine. He may use Pinot Noirs from different sections in such a manner that in combination vintage distinctions are all but obliterated.

Many Spanish and Italian producers have in the past been exceedingly lax about affixing correct vintage dates to their wines. (The situation in this respect is improving, especially in Italy.) It didn't matter much, because their climates and winemaking practices combined to make the producer's job easy. Although the fixing of vintage labels has always been tightly controlled in the United States, the same conditions, roughly, have obtained for California producers—and consumers.

There are a couple of exceptions to this rule. First, as California wineries produce more and more single-location and even single-vineyard wines, and so designate them—the practice, though still not widespread, is growing—vintage information will become nearly as important as it is for the premium producers of France and Germany—"nearly," because extremes still will not obtain. When all the grapes come from one vineyard, the weather in that vineyard is very important. Second, the better the wine is, the more important vintage information is. When one considers the 100 percent varietal Cabernet Sauvignons, Chardonnays, and Pinot Noirs of the better California producers, vintages play an increasingly important role. Such thoroughbreds only reach the heights that they can attain when everything, including the vintage, conspires together.

In addition, even though vintage information is not so important as in France or Germany, there is no question that some years in California are better than others. Thus a California vintage chart— based on a high score of 10—is included here.

California:	Recent Vintages	
	Red	White
1968	9	X
1969	7	X
1970	9	X
1971	8	7
1972	6	6
1973	8	8
1974	9	9
1975	8	8
1976	8	7
1977	8	7

To use the chart effectively, one should bear the following in mind: (1) "Red" means Cabernet Sauvignon particularly and big reds generally. (2) "White" effectively means Chardonnay. Other California whites with the exception of such sweet wines as late harvest Johannisberg Riesling should be drunk young, as should lesser Chardonnays.

Finally, no vintage chart can do justice to any one vintage. Good winemakers can make acceptable wine in a bad year. Bad wines are made in good years. Too many variables are at work for a vintage chart to be more than an elementary guide.

STORAGE

The section on vintages gives a person interested in "laying down" some wines in a "cellar" many clues. Depending on the depth of one's purse, one should try to lay down good quality. That also means wines from good producers—Cabernet Sauvignons, Zinfandels, Petite Sirahs, possible Pinot Noirs; and, as whites, Chardonnays and some late harvest Rieslings. A good cellar also will include a selection of sparkling and fortified wines and plenty of wines bought not to lay away but to drink now: quality jugs, rosés, Chenin Blancs, dry Rieslings, etc.

It is odd, but many people who start to build up a wine cellar forget that wines are to be *drunk.* They have lives; even the best are not immortal, except in people's memories. The liquids in the bottles change steadily, and eventually the change is for the worse.

One stores certain wines to ensure a supply at a price one can afford and to give them a chance to age in stable conditions. But this aging is not to be prolonged indefinitely. Most California wines should be drunk as young as possible. Few whites will repay any cellaring at all. Even good Chardonnays should be carefully watched. After three or four years many, especially if not carefully stored, will start to oxidize and deteriorate. Only the very best will repay much longer storage, and only a few will last as long as ten years. (The chart lists no ranking for Chardonnays before 1971 for that reason: if you don't have them, don't buy them, even if you find them.)

Big reds need longer age than whites and will last longer. But only the very biggest Cabernet Sauvignons are not ready within five years of being bottled and will last more than fifteen years, unless stored under ideal conditions.

A word about a cellar: Few people have a traditional wine cellar, and not many more have access to a cool basement. It does not matter too much. Provided that the storage area is dark, quiet, still, and not susceptible to rapid or frequent temperature changes, anywhere, even a closet, will make an excellent "cellar." Ideally, the temperature should be a constant 55 degrees Fahrenheit or thereabouts. More important than the specific temperature is a constant temperature. Wine will age more quickly at a temperature higher than 60, but if the temperature is steady, the wine will age well. Wine does not like upsets. If left to itself, it will do very well in less than ideal conditions.

Finally, when you buy to lay away, buy young and buy well.

SERVING AND DRINKING

Much has been written about how to enjoy wine, and much that is written and said is sententious rubbish. The idea is only to enjoy it, period. Much of the ritual attached to drinking wine is nonsense, and it should be adhered to only insofar as it contributes to the drinker's enjoyment of the wine.

This is not the forum to discuss how to drink and serve wine, but below are listed some elementary suggestions that, if followed, should contribute to your enjoyment of U.S. wines.

Glasses

Glasses should be clean (wash dirty glasses in clean hot water only; if you must use a detergent, rinse the glasses very thoroughly; dry with a clean cloth), stemmed (so that drinkers may hold the stem and not warm or smear the bowls with their hands), and made of the best-quality clear glass or crystal you can afford (so that you can see the wine to its best advantage). Drinking wine is very much a visual as well as an olfactory and taste experience.

Table wines should be served in goblet-shaped glasses. The surface of the wine will be exposed to the air; the curl of the glass will funnel the aroma up to the drinker. Sparkling wines should be served in tulip- or flute-shaped glasses, which preserve the sparkle in the wine longer than does the traditional and less effective saucer-shaped glass.

Serving Temperature

Different types of wine show best at different temperatures. The following table suggests a temperature range:

Big red wines	65° F
Rosés and light reds	55° F
Dry whites	50° F
Sparkling wines	45° F
Sweet whites	40° F

These temperatures should not be followed slavishly; they are guides only. But they should help rectify the tendency most people have to chill dry whites too much and to serve dry reds too warm.

The often-mentioned "room temperature" is not a heated-room temperature.

Breathing

"Breathing" is a matter of controversy. But it is generally agreed that young wines will taste a lot better than they would otherwise if they are opened an hour or two before being served. Older wines also will benefit from a period of breathing, but the older a wine is, the less breathing it can stand. Very old wines should be decanted and poured almost immediately after they have been opened. Like humans, wines of great age become very fragile and sudden exposure to air can rob them of their refined strength very quickly.

As in all things pertaining to wine, there are no hard and fast rules about breathing. Unless the wines are very young, when as much as three hours and a decanting will do them good, one should be watchful.

A FINAL WORD

Don't expect your wine to be at its best if you buy it, carry it home, open it, and serve it. Even the youngest wine will show better if it is given a rest before it is served, a day or two at least. The older the wine, the more time it needs to settle and recover itself after any movement. This is especially the case if a wine is old enough to have developed a sediment and needs to be decanted off the sediment before being served.

FURTHER READING

The best way to find out about the wines of the United States is to drink them, and certainly there could not be more pleasant research. Unfortunately, however, shortage of funds, lack of time, and/or limits to one's capacity usually conspire to prevent the sort of research that one might choose to initiate.

The next best method is to visit wineries and try some of their wines *in situ*. Many wineries welcome visitors, daily or by appointment. The Sunset book mentioned below is an excellent source for information about California. Wherever you wish to go, a phone call ahead will save a possibly wasted trip if you do not know for certain that a particular winery is open to the public. As a rule of thumb, the very smallest and some of the very largest—Gallo, for example—are not open.

Finally, one can supplement tasting by reading, superficially or in as great a depth as desired. For current information, a number of newsletters are published on a regular basis. Two of the best are *Robert Finigan's Private Guide to Wines* (100 Bush Street, San Francisco, CA 94104) and *The Connoisseurs' Guide to California Wine* (PO Box 11120, San Francisco, CA 94101). Two attractive and informative magazines are *Wine World* (15101 Keswick Street, Van Nuys, CA 91405), a bimonthly, and the monthly *Vintage* (139 East 57th Street, New York, NY 10022).

Many wineries put out free newsletters—chiefly, of course, about their own wines. If one particularly likes the wines of a winery, it is worth inquiring if that favorite winery offers such a service. The most information, especially about vineyard and winery practices, and least self-serving, is that written by Sam J. Sebastiani of Sebastiani Vineyards (PO Box AA, 389 Fourth Street, Sonoma, CA 95476).

There are many winetasting societies, most of which involve high-sounding titles, fancy outfits, and other paraphernalia. Wine snobs abound in such rarefied environments. One national organization, Les Amis du Vin (2302 Perkins Place, Silver Spring, MD 20910), is a happy exception. It sponsors many local chapters, and membership entitles one to discounts on specially selected wines at participating stores and to a subscription to a very informative magazine, *Wine*.

Finally, there are books—far too many to list except very selectively:

The classic reference book is *Alexis Lichine's New Encyclopedia of Wines and Spirits* (New York: Knopf, 1974). This encyclopedia lives up to its title and covers the wines of the world. Less overwhelming in detail, but still very useful, are *Frank Schoonmaker's Encyclopedia of Wine*, seventh edition, by Julius Wile (New York: Hastings House, 1978), and *Grossman's Guide to Wines, Beer, and*

Spirits, sixth revised edition by Harriet Lembeck (New York: Scribner, 1978).

Hugh Johnson's *Wine,* revised edition (New York: Simon & Schuster, 1974), is a superbly written survey of the world's wines. The same author's *The World Atlas of Wine,* revised edition (New York: Simon & Schuster, 1978), is to the wine enthusiast what Rand McNally is to the driver: an essential geographic guide.

The Wines of America, second edition, revised, by Leon D. Adams (New York: McGraw-Hill, 1978), is a first-rate survey of the whole industry. Adams's knowledge of the history of the wine industry is unmatched. He has traveled tirelessly for years and made notes about everything. *The Signet Book of American Wine* by Peter Quimme (New York: New American Library, 1975) is one of a series of useful paperback surveys of wines and wine drinking.

For California, the most useful books are *The California Wine Book* by Bob Thompson and Hugh Johnson (New York: Morrow, 1976) and *California Wine Country* by the Editors of Sunset Books and Sunset Magazine (Menlo Park, CA.: Lane, 1978). The latter, a paperback, contains excellent maps and instructions for reaching particular wineries.

Of course, the very best reading of all is the label of the wine you are about to drink.

INDEX